Speaking God's Word

A Book of Lessons and Confessions
Volume II

Minister Gloria Moody

Speaking God's Word

Speaking God's Word: A Book of Lessons and Confessions Volume II

Copyright © 2016 by Minister Gloria Moody

ISBN-10: 0-692-70534-1

ISBN-13: 978-0-692-70534-6

Scripture quotations taken from the Amplified® Bible, Copyright © 1987, 2015 by The Lockman Foundation. Used by permission.(www.Lockman.org)

Scripture quotations marked KJV are from the King James Version of the Bible.

Scripture quotations are taken from the Holy Bible, New Living Translation, copyright ©1996, 2004, 2007, 2013, 2015 by Tyndale House Foundation. Used by permission of Tyndale House Publishers, Inc., Carol Stream, Illinois 60188. All rights reserved.

Scripture quotations marked (TLB) are taken from The Living Bible copyright © 1971. Used by permission of Tyndale House Publishers, Inc., Carol Stream, Illinois 60188. All rights reserved.

Scripture quotations from THE MESSAGE. Copyright © by Eugene H. Peterson 1993, 1994, 1995, 1996, 2000, 2001, 2002. Used by permission of NavPress. All rights reserved. Represented by Tyndale House Publishers, Inc.

Scripture taken from the New King James Version®. Copyright © 1982 by Thomas Nelson. Used by permission. All rights reserved.

This book was printed in the United States of America.

Authored and Published by Gloria Moody

www.confessinggodsword.org

www.speakinggodsword.org

*T*able of *C*ontents

*D*edication

This book is dedicated to:

Every Born Again Believer – who is joined together by Jesus Christ, as well as all of the Brothers and Sisters who enjoyed Volume I.

All of the Believers and Partners who are associated with Confessing God's Word Ministries.

My parents, Luvert and Willie Mae Listenbee, and my sister Joyce (Listenbee) Bennett, all of whom have gone on to be with the Lord. I believe that the incomparable support, encouragement and unconditional love that I received from them throughout my life has heightened my sensitivity and ability to really understand the love of God, and to know that God is Love.

Finally, to my husband, Ezell Moody, our children and grandchildren, our sisters and brothers, nieces, nephews and cousins, all of whom I love deeply.

Acknowledgements

I give all praise, honor and glory to Jesus Christ, my Lord and Savior, and to my Father, Almighty God. I am so grateful for the prompting from the Holy Spirit to complete this book. It has been a love walk between us and I could not have done it without His inspiration, clarification and revelation that is presented in these pages.

I deeply appreciate my sisters Beverly Johnson and Sandra Green. Thank you both for your prayers, love and advice. Much love to you both!

Finally, I give thanks to my wonderful husband, Ezell Moody, who is always a constant source of strength, encouragement and support. Thank you, Dearest, for editing and critiquing my work. I thank you so much for your patience and love as well. I appreciate you, I love you, and thank God for you. You are simply the best!

*E*ndorsements

"The principle of confession has been a largely misunderstood and widely criticized subject in the Body of Christ. Gloria Moody takes confession and makes it palatable to our minds and spirits by simplifying the process. She takes the Scriptures and personalizes them into modern everyday vernacular, thereby teaching even the youngest of Christians how to confess the Word of God. An excellent book to empower someone to learn how to speak the Word only!"

Hiram Gomez
President / Founder
Triumphant Living International

"I strongly believe that God has given Minister Gloria Moody a mandate for such a time as this, to ignite the prayer confessions in the lives of His people. As I read *Speaking God's Word*, it was like reading the Book of Psalms, penned by the fingers of Gloria, in the 21st Century.

The *Book* has the anointing of the Holy Spirit, breathing on every stroke and declaring His faithfulness and promises. The prophetic flows through every word, in poetic style. The scriptures will ignite your faith, prayers and hope. Reciting these confessions will change the lives of all those who feast on declaring these powerful words."

La Vada D. Humphrey
Minister, Motivational Speaker, Author

"When we begin to understand the power and purpose of speaking the Word properly as it is presented in this book, we become the victors that God desires us to be. What an awesome tool for our spiritual development!"

Dr. Stephanie C.
International Speaker, Author and Coach

"After a combined total of almost 40 years in ministry, my wife, Pastor Staci and I have discovered one truth about the body of believers and it is this: we continue to live beneath our privileges as part of God's royal priesthood. So many times we accept all that the enemy attempts to do in our lives with little to no resistance. Moreover, we rarely rely on the power the Lord has given us through our ability to frame our world with our words. This is why we are praising God for the release of *Volume II of Speaking God's Word: A Book of Lessons and Confessions.*

This book provides the believer with lessons and practical examples of how to apply the word of God to every situation in your life. We believe that God walks the earth listening for His word. The bible tells us in Numbers 23:19 that, "God is not a man that he should lie." He does not change His mind, so if He said it that settles it. This book, in the hands of the believer, becomes more than just a collection of words on pages. It is a weapon of mass destruction to the enemy's camp."

God bless you Pastor Gloria Moody!

Yours in Christ,

Dr. Damen M. Bennett, Pastor
Fresh Oil Ministries
Gary, Indiana

"Outstanding array of the Word of God that addresses many areas of our lives. This work by Gloria is something that I believe every Believer in the Lord Jesus Christ would greatly benefit from. It also serves as a tremendous daily devotional to begin, work through and end your day with!"

Osazee O. Thompson
Goal Performance Coach, Speaker, Author of Precision
Purpose: Enjoying the Signature Life You Were Born
to Live!

"Many in the Church are seeking ways in which to deepen their relationship with the Lord through prayer, as well as gain understanding and techniques on inspiring and motivating a team of intercessors.

I believe this book is an excellent guide for anyone who wants to pray anointed and powerful prayers, backed up in scripture. The scriptures are clear about the Father's desire to be in relationship with His children. One way to do that is to effectively enter into prayer and intercession. In this way, we learn to recognize His heart, hear His voice, and discern how to act upon the prompts He gives us. *Speaking God's Word* is a vehicle that gives instructions on how to accomplish that goal."

Apostle Camille A.D. Mathews

"Gloria Moody is a God-ordained Author, Minister and Woman of God. I believe that her intimate relationship with God is evident in both Volumes of *Speaking God's Word*. Each page is packed with powerful words of faith, encouragement and revelation. This is an awesome book that will definitely bless every reader."

Sasha M. Brown
Daughter

*F*oreword

Pastor Gloria Moody's new book *Speaking God's Word: A Book of Lessons and Confessions Volume II* is beautifully founded on the Word of God. Speaking God's Word is a dialogue of love and empowerment between the Author and the Creator.

This *Book* is birth out of a deep relationship of Faith and Obedience between the two. As you read this book you hear the Word of Faith being spoken, for the building and development of God's people. *Speaking God's Word* imparts a love for the Father and stirs your Faith to confess His Word on a daily basis to release Miracles in your life.

Apostle Otis J. Caldwell
Kingdom Faith Ministries Intl.
Chicago, IL.

*I*ntroduction

As Born Again Believers, we have a mandate to keep God's Word in our mouths. Joshua 1:8 says *"This Book of the Law shall not depart from your mouth, but you shall meditate in it day and night, that you may observe to do according to all that is written in it. For then you will make your way prosperous, and then you will have good success."* In other words, as Children of God and Citizens of the Kingdom of God, we do not have the right to just let anything come out of our mouths. We were created with the power of death and life in our tongues (Proverbs 18:21). So as we move forward and continue to expect the best in our lives, we must remember that our success will be in direct proportion to not only how we are using our faith, but also by the words that we are speaking.

We have been given many other promises and commands throughout the scriptures concerning our words and their power. We have the power to make decrees (Job 22:28). So when we decree the Word of God, God says that His Word has enough power to fulfill or perform Itself because with God, nothing is ever impossible (Luke 1:37). Heaven and earth shall pass away, but His Words shall not (according to Mark 13:31). We can therefore always depend on God, our Father, and His Word!

Deuteronomy 30:19 says "*I call heaven and earth to record this day against you, that I have set before you, life and death, blessing and cursing: therefore, choose life, that both thou and thy seed may live.*" With the power and responsibility that we have with our words, we are urged to keep evil or worthless words out of our mouths (Ephesians 4:29). Instead, let the words of our mouths and the meditation of our hearts be acceptable in God's sight (Psalm 19:14).

In 2008, the Holy Spirit imparted in my heart to share with others, and specifically to the Body of Christ, the importance of speaking God's Word. I heeded the call, and wrote *Speaking God's Word: A Book of Lessons and Confessions Volume I.*

Volume II covers the remaining seven areas. I continued to receive revelation on the scriptures during the eight years between *Volume I* and now, hence the subject areas are expanded in *Volume II.* These lessons and confessions are the result of close communication and impartation from the Holy Spirit. As I listened, I received and I wrote. It is my sincerest desire that the reader will blessed and encouraged by the lessons and confessions found in this book. I hope that you will use it as the tool for which it was written – a handbook to be read aloud, as you receive revelation, insight and clarity.

In His Service,
Gloria Moody

Seeing and Hearing

Seeing and Hearing

1 Corinthians 2:9

But as it is written, Eye hath not seen, nor ear heard, neither have entered into the heart of man, the things which God hath prepared for them that love him. (KJV)

I love You, God! I trust Your Word, Father. What You have already done for me – what is already prepared for me – is more than I've ever imagined. Help me to hear You more clearly with my spiritual ears. Let me be in tune with the frequency of Your Voice, and Yours alone. Open my spiritual eyes so that I can see beyond what is appearing in the natural. Father, help me to know that everything You have promised is already prepared for me. It's already done in the spirit realm, awaiting my call.

In Jesus's Name, I decree that my imagination is expanding right now. My capacity to receive what You have prepared for me is increasing daily. I think BIG, Father, because You are the opulent, regenerating, overflowing, replenishing, and abundant God of the magnificent. With excitement and anticipation, I receive in my spirit everything that You have already made, especially for me, with my name on it. I now await physical manifestation.

Hallelujah, my God, I thank You for what You've done for me. Thank You for loving me. I love You too! Thank You providing for every one of my needs, and even knowing what they are ahead of time. Thank You for always hearing me and always answering my prayers. Thank You for giving me the desires of my heart. Thank You for being El Shaddai, the Self-Sufficient, Almighty God. There is none other like You. Hallelujah!

Seeing and Hearing

John 10:27

My sheep hear my voice, and I know them, and they follow me. (KJV)

The sheep that are My own hear and are listening to My voice; and I know them, and they follow Me. (AMP)

I belong to You, Jesus! I am one of Your very own. Wow! Thank You for the privilege. What an honor, Jesus. Thank You for calling me into Your Kingdom. Thank You for choosing me. I don't take it lightly. I desire to do all that You instruct me to do. I will not listen to a stranger's voice. Nor will I follow any doctrines of the devil. I am listening for Your Voice all the time. Yours is the Voice that I follow.

I turn a deaf ear to the devil for he has nothing to do with me or my future. He is defeated and under my feet! I refuse to listen to his lies or suggestions anymore. Praise the Lord! I follow the Voice of the Good Shepherd, Jesus Christ. He is the Author and Finisher of my faith. I will not hesitate to follow Your leadings, Lord Jesus.

Speaking God's Word

I choose to hear God's Word and act on it. I hasten to do what You tell me to do, at all times. As I do, I believe and expect what the Word of God promises me. I absolutely trust You always for my highest good, and I will always give You the highest praise! Hallelujah!

The Will of God is foremost on my mind. The Word of God is forever in my heart and in my mouth. Thank You for knowing and understanding me, Jesus. Thank You for loving me as well. You are the Bread of Life. You are my Lord and Savior. You are my Shepherd and I shall not want. It does not matter what others think, because I belong to You. You are the only One who matters and I will listen for Your Majestic Voice and follow You always!

Seeing and Hearing

James 1:22

But be ye doers of the word, and not hearers only, deceiving your own selves. (KJV)

But don't just listen to God's word. You must do what it says. Otherwise, you are only fooling yourselves. (NLT)

I am not only a hearer of Your Word, Father, but I am a doer of Your Word as well. I choose to live the abundant life that Jesus came to give me. Therefore, I do what You tell me to do. I fast and I pray. I tithe and I thrive. I sow and I reap. I give and I receive. I forgive as I have been forgiven. I love and I am loved. I give thanks to You, Father God, for Your Goodness!

Hallelujah! My faith comes by hearing Your Word, Father God. Hearing what You have said about me – who and what I am in You – causes my faith to increase. As I grow in the knowledge of Jesus Christ, my faith continues to increase. Hearing the Gospel, the uncompromising Word of God, is what I seek. I will not be deceived any longer. I accept nothing less than the Word of God to operate in my life.

Speaking God's Word

Your Rhema Word causes me to have increased faith. I do what You tell me to do, Father God. My faith is in You!

I plant Your Word as seed into my heart. As a result, the Truth of who I am in You grows and develops in me. I am indeed a new creation. I am Your Beloved. Hearing the promises that You have made for me and my life cause me to see things differently. I no longer depend on the distorted world view to dictate my way of living. My expectation for everything is from You and You alone. I allow the Word of God to mold and shape my life. I look to You Father God, as my Source and my Provider. You are my Creator and my Sustainer. I give You alone all the Glory and all the Honor, in Jesus's Name!

Seeing and Hearing

2 Corinthians 4:17-18

For our light affliction, which is but for a moment, worketh for us a far more exceeding and eternal weight of glory; While we look not at the things which are seen, but at the things which are not seen: for the things which are seen are temporal; but the things which are not seen are eternal. (KJV)

Glory to God! I look towards the eternal. Afflictions that may be appearing are temporary because You, Lord, promised to deliver me from them all. What I cannot see is just as real as what I can see. Whatever is appearing in my life now, whatever I can see now, is temporal and temporary. It is subject to change. It came to pass. I will longer focus on any storms that may come through, because they did not come to stay. I will no longer have any fear, Father because You always provide a way of escape for me. I will keep my eyes on You and on Your Word, only. My way is already made. Hallelujah!

Glory to God! I no longer trust in appearances. The devil has deceived the whole world, but I now have revelation of the Truth. I will no longer be discouraged, saddened or confused by his lies. I will not be swayed by what I see because what I now see is not the real for me. My reality is what the Word says about me – good and plenty. I look to the eternal, the realm of the unseen, for my harvest. I keep my eyes on our Covenant, Father, for my wealthy place, my inheritance and my good. Hallelujah!

Glory to God! The Blessing of the Lord is on me. I have been redeemed from the curse. Any lack, pain, sickness, disease, or any other evidence of the curse is a lie. I will no longer be manipulated by the deceptions of the devil. I refuse to allow appearances to control me. They are temporary inconveniences and fleeting setbacks, that do indeed change. With a grateful heart, I thank You, Father. Hallelujah!

Seeing and Hearing

1 Samuel 3:10

And the LORD came, and stood, and called as at other times, Samuel, Samuel. Then Samuel answered, Speak; for thy servant heareth. (KJV)

Then GOD came and stood before him exactly as before, calling out, "Samuel! Samuel!" Samuel answered, "Speak. I'm your servant, ready to listen." (The Message)

Then the LORD came and stood and called as at the previous times, "Samuel! Samuel!" Then Samuel answered, "Speak, for Your servant is listening." (AMP)

I, like Samuel, hear You, Lord! I am listening. I long to hear Your Voice. I love to hear Your Words of Encouragement. I await Your Comfort when I am weary. I listen for Your Triumphant Voice of Victory to fill my heart with gladness! I appreciate Your Confidence in me. I love to hear Your Sweet, Calm Voice. Thank You, God, for Your Instructions and Directions.

Lord, Your Child is listening. I'm ready to serve You in every way. I am Your Ambassador. I am Your Special Envoy.

Speaking God's Word

I go where You need me to go. I do what You want me to do. I handle Kingdom Business as You direct me. I am not ashamed of the Gospel of Jesus Christ and I share it with everyone I meet. Thank You for the privilege of representing You, Father.

I trust You, Lord. Thank You for trusting me to do Your Work and to be Your Voice here on the earth. Thank You for anointing me with the ability to pursue, overtake, and recover all. Continue to teach me Your Ways and reveal to me Your Secrets, Father. Show me how to represent You more and more. As Your Child, I listen continually for Your Revelations. I have ears to hear. One Word from You is all I need. Hallelujah! Speak! Your Servant is listening!

Seeing and Hearing

2 Corinthians 4:3-4

But if our gospel be hid, it is hid to them that are lost: In whom the god of this world hath blinded the minds of them which believe not, lest the light of the glorious gospel of Christ, who is the image of God, should shine unto them. (KJV)

If the Good News we preach is hidden behind a veil, it is hidden only from people who are perishing. Satan, who is the god of this world, has blinded the minds of those who don't believe. They are unable to see the glorious light of the Good News. They don't understand this message about the glory of Christ, who is the exact likeness of God. (NLT)

Thank You, Lord. I have been redeemed! Thank You, God, for the Gospel of Jesus Christ. I am no longer blinded by the god of this world – Satan. He is the father of lies and has deceived the whole world. Praise God, the veil of darkness has been lifted from my mind. Hallelujah! I can see clearly now. I will never again be tricked by the devil. I keep my eyes on the Glorious Light of Jesus Christ. I am not ashamed of the Gospel. I will forever proclaim to the world that Jesus Christ is Lord!

Speaking God's Word

Father God, thank You for Jesus. He is my Savior, my Deliverer and my Redeemer. Thank You for making a way out for those who are lost and destined to perish in hell. Let them know that in Your Kingdom, all is well. Thank You for Your Mercy that is fresh every day. I shall proclaim to all – that Jesus Christ is the Way.

Father, help me to be a witness to those who are still blinded by the enemy. Let those blinders be removed, so that they too can see the light, and receive the good news. Lord, let all whom I come in contact with, see Your Light in me. Let me be a carrier of the Gospel in my words, deeds and my activity. Father, let them know that You alone are God, awaiting them with open arms. Amen!

Seeing and Hearing

Psalm 27:13-14

I had fainted, unless I had believed to see the goodness of the LORD in the land of the living. Wait on the LORD: be of good courage, and he shall strengthen thine heart: wait, I say, on the LORD. (KJV)

Hallelujah! I shall live and see the goodness of the Lord, every day. I will not die. I will indeed see the manifestation of every one of my prayers. I shall receive and experience all of my desires. Praise the Lord! I shall reach my destiny. I will not faint. Thank You, Father, for restoring me and renewing my strength. I shall run and not be weary. Glory to God!

Hallelujah! I am of good courage. I am confident because of You. My heart is strengthened because I trust in the Lord. I am bold as a lion. I am encouraged day by day. The joy of the Lord is my strength. I will not turn back. I shall live to see the goodness of God. My latter days shall be greater than my former. My better and best is yet to come. My good and very good is on the way. My God! Thank You for saving the best for me. Thank You for girding me up, so that I can see

Speaking God's Word

all of Your Goodness in my life, from this moment on. You are so Awesome!

Hallelujah! I believe I shall see the goodness of the Lord today. Something good is going to happen for me today. I shall be blessed indeed. Bless me, bless me today, my God. Show up for me today, my God. Manifest Your Goodness for me today, my God. I am determined to hold on – the best is yet to come. I shall stay strong – for I know it won't be long. I thank You for Your Awesome Promises and the manifestation of Your Magnificence in my life, for all to see. You are the Supernatural God of the Miraculous. All glory to You, my Father!

Seeing and Hearing

2 Corinthians 3:17-18

For the Lord is the Spirit, and wherever the Spirit of the Lord is, there is freedom. So all of us who have had that veil removed can see and reflect the glory of the Lord. And the Lord—who is the Spirit—makes us more and more like him as we are changed into his glorious image. (NLT)

Now the Lord is the Spirit, and where the Spirit of the Lord is, there is liberty [emancipation from bondage, true freedom]. And we all, with unveiled face, continually seeing as in a mirror the glory of the Lord, are progressively being transformed into His image from [one degree of] glory to [even more] glory, which comes from the Lord, [who is] the Spirit. (AMP)

I am free, Praise God! I am free to be all that You have created me to be. I can do everything that I was born to do, through the Spirit of the Lord abiding in me. The devil has been defeated and has no more hold on me. I thank God that I am free indeed. I decree and declare that I will never ever be bound again to any person, situation or circumstance. Glory Hallelujah!

Change me, Father. Mold me and shape me so that Your Glory is reflected in every area of my life. Thank You for lifting the veil of ignorance from me. I no longer walk in darkness. I am not deceived anymore. Through the Blood of Jesus, I have been bought back. I have been set free from lack. I am financially free to be as wealthy as I want to be. I have been redeemed from sickness. I am free to be as healthy as You created me to be. I am free and the Blessing is on me. Glory Hallelujah!

Whom the Son has set free is free indeed. Praise the Lord! I am liberated from the yoke of bondage. I am unrestrained. I am released from all chains. I am free. I will never ever be bound again. I am not the same. I can now walk freely and speedily towards my destiny. I accept Your Glory, God, to resonate in and through me. I praise Your Holy Name! Hallelujah!

Seeing and Hearing

And the LORD said to Moses, "Has the LORD's arm been shortened? Now you shall see whether what I say will happen to you or not." (NKJV)

The LORD said to Moses, "Is the LORD'S hand (ability, power) limited (short, inadequate)? You shall see now whether My word will come to pass for you or not." (AMP)

Then the Lord said to Moses, "When did I become weak? Now you shall see whether my word comes true or not!" (TLB)

Glory Hallelujah! There is no weakness in You, Lord God. There is nothing inadequate about You either. Your Power and Ability have not diminished in any way. You are the Alpha and the Omega, the Everlasting and Eternal God, who cannot lie. There is nothing too hard for You and Your Word has no limitation. There is absolutely nothing that Your Word cannot accomplish. Praise the Lord!

I believe every Word that You have spoken, Father. If You said it, I have no doubt that it shall come to pass. What you have spoken to me shall manifest in my life. I receive Your

Speaking God's Word

Promises, for all things are possible with You. Every Word that You have decreed shall show up indeed. I expect a performance of those things which You have said to me.

Hallelujah! Your Voice is powerful, Lord God, and full of majesty. Your Word shall not return to You void. Neither shall Your Word return to me without fulfillment. With You, Almighty God, nothing is ever impossible and all of Your Words are full of power. I have no doubt that Your Word is true and shall manifest for me. I am blessed by the Best. Thank You, Father God. Glory, Glory, Glory! You are the Great God Jehovah!

Seeing and Hearing

Proverbs 29:18

Where there is no vision, the people perish: but he that keepeth the law, happy is he. (KJV)

Where there is no vision [no revelation of God and His word], the people are unrestrained; But happy and blessed is he who keeps the law [of God]. (AMPC)

If people can't see what God is doing, they stumble all over themselves; But when they attend to what he reveals, they are most blessed. (The Message)

Hallelujah! I will not perish because I have the vision for my life as one of God's very own. I have revelation of God's Plan of Redemption for His Children. I respect and follow the laws of the land. More importantly, I respect and follow the laws of the Kingdom and I am happy, free and blessed.

Thank You for Your Heavenly Vision for my life, Father. I can see that my future looks bright. I shall indeed be fruitful in the Kingdom of God here in the earth. I am being restored and repaid everything Satan has stolen from me and my family. Health and wholeness is my status. I expect everlasting blessings to overtake me in all areas of my life. I ask and I receive because You promised to withhold no good thing from me, Father God.

You give me the desires of my heart because I always delight myself in You, Lord God. I will remain upright in my relationship with You, Father and my inheritance shall be forever. I am blessed with Faithful Abraham and wealth and riches are in my house forever. Everything I do prospers because You teach me to profit. Your Blessing brings great wealth to me without difficulty. You have prepared everything for me that I will ever need for life and godliness. To all of this I say Thank You, Father!

Seeing and Hearing

NOTES & REFLECTIONS
COMMENTS & YOUR THOUGHTS
ON
SEEING AND HEARING

_____

_____

_____

_____

_____

_____

_____

_____

_____

_____

_____

_____

23

Speaking God's Word

_____

_____

_____

_____

_____

_____

_____

_____

_____

_____

_____

_____

_____

_____

_____

_____

Love, Joy and Peace

Love, Joy and Peace

John 14:21

He who has My commandments and keeps them, it is he who loves Me. And he who loves Me will be loved by My Father, and I will love him and manifest Myself to him. (NKJV)

I follow Your Commandments because I love You, Father. I do what You have told me to do. Thank You for loving me, Jesus. I keep Your Commandments and follow Your Instructions. I forgive those who have hurt me or wronged me in any way. I do not take offense. I take no anxious thoughts about my future. I give first, then receive. I seek Your Kingdom first, and expect that everything I will ever need, want or desire will be added to me.

Thank You Father, for manifesting Yourself in my life. You always answer my prayers. Your Favor is on me all the time. I speak Your Word and You make sure that It does not return to me void. Your Word always produces in my life. You always open doors and avenues for me. You make ways out of nowhere for me. You always breakthrough for me, and I am filled with gratitude and praise. Thank You, Lord God!

Speaking God's Word

I praise You, Jesus. Your Yoke Breaking, Burden Removing Anointing is upon me always. You are the God of the Miraculous in my life. I cast my cares onto You and You take care of everything concerning me. You increase me more and more, me and my family. Your Supernatural Activity is obvious in every area of my life, and I am forever thankful, Father. You love me and I love You. Such sweet melody. Selah!

Love, Joy and Peace

Psalm 35:27

Let them shout for joy, and be glad, that favour my righteous cause: yea, let them say continually, Let the LORD be magnified, which hath pleasure in the prosperity of his servant. (KJV)

Let them shout for joy and rejoice, who favor my vindication and want what is right for me; Let them say continually, "Let the LORD be magnified, who delights and takes pleasure in the prosperity of His servant." (AMP)

Hallelujah, I shout for joy and I am glad about it! I shout now, even before the evidence comes. I know it shall arrive because You promised. Hallelujah! My soul bubbles over acclaiming the good news. I am prosperous indeed because it pleases You. Let the Lord be magnified at all times. You are God alone. I praise Your Holy Name!

Hallelujah, I shout for joy and I'm exceedingly grateful. Not only am I Your Servant but I am Your Child. Praise the Lord! Thank You for wishing above all things that I prosper. It is so wonderful that You receive pleasure from my overflowing abundance. Lord, I thank You for being my Source and providing channels of good for me. I lift You up and magnify You. I shout for joy. Every day is a marvelous day that the Lord my God has made. I rejoice and I am glad about it. You, my God, are so worthy to be praised!

Hallelujah, I shout for joy. I'm extremely excited. I favor Your Righteous Cause. I want what You want, Lord. Your Agenda is foremost on my mind. You promised that all of Your Grace is upon me, which is indeed my sufficiency. Such pleasure You give me. I always have enough to do good works. I exalt You, my Loving Father! You are so wonderful to me! It is all for Your Honor and Your Glory!

Love, Joy and Peace

Isaiah 26:3

Thou wilt keep him in perfect peace, whose mind is stayed on thee: because he trusteth in thee. (KJV)

He will keep in perfect peace all those who trust in him, whose thoughts turn often to the Lord! (TLB)

You keep me in perfect peace, Lord, as I keep my mind stayed on You. Lord God, I simply trust You. When frustrations come, I think of You. You remind me that this too shall pass. I look to You, Father, for perfect peace that passes all understanding. As I do, each and every time without exception, You wrap me in Your Arms and comfort me with Your Peace. You make my problems seem small and the challenges I face seem insignificant. You never let me down. You never disappoint me. You are an Awesome God!

Perfect peace belongs to me because I keep my mind stayed on Thee. You are the Great Omniscient God who knows the solutions, and You solve all my problems. I trust You, Lord, for You have all the answers.

Speaking God's Word

You are the great Omnipresent God, ahead of me all the time. You penetrate every obstacle for me, smooth out all the rough edges, and straighten every crooked place in my life. You alone give me peace and keep me serene. I love You for who You are to me. Hallelujah!

Your Greatness, Your Goodness and Your Mercy cover my soul with ease. I do not allow the events of the day to get me down in any way. I resist the temptation to wallow in despair. My thoughts are focused on You and I have not a care. My emotions remain calm. My feelings are intact. I relax in You. I rejoice in You. I find happiness in You. As You trust me, I trust You. Thank You Jehovah Shalom – my God of peace and much, much more. You are all that. You are the One whom I adore. Selah!

Love, Joy and Peace

Zephaniah 3:17

The LORD thy God in the midst of thee is mighty; he will save, he will rejoice over thee with joy; he will rest in his love, he will joy over thee with singing. (KJV)

The Lord your God is in the midst of you, a Mighty One, a Savior [Who saves]! He will rejoice over you with joy; He will rest [in silent satisfaction] and in His love He will be silent and make no mention [of past sins, or even recall them]; He will exult over you with singing. (AMPC)

Oh Mighty One in the midst of me, thank You for saving me. I am pleased that You have joy and rejoice over me. It is so awesome that You love me and find me to be a source of joy to You. Thank You for finding satisfaction in me, just as I am. My God – my goodness! El Elyon, what a Mighty God You are. My focus is always on You, Lord God. My heart is filled with gratitude, thanks and praise. Hallelujah!

Thank You for not bringing up my past life of sin and error. Thank You for not having any record of it. Instead, You have recorded me in the Lamb's Book of Life. Glory to Jesus! I learn from You, Father. If You are silent about my past, I will not recall it either. If You remember no more those things that happened before my new birth, neither will I. Thank You for creating me to be worthy of Your Joy. Hallelujah!

As You rejoice over me for being Yours, I rejoice over You for being mine. You are the Protector of my soul. I lift You up. I magnify You. I worship and adore You. I bless Your Holy Name. I welcome Your Presence as I sing praises unto You in all that I do. Your Presence is what I seek. It overwhelms me and keeps me meek. It lets me know that You alone are God. You alone are so worthy to be praised. Thank You Father. Hallelujah!

Love, Joy and Peace

Romans 8:37-40

Nay, in all these things we are more than conquerors through him that loved us. For I am persuaded, that neither death, nor life, nor angels, nor principalities, nor powers, nor things present, nor things to come, Nor height, nor depth, nor any other creature, shall be able to separate us from the love of God, which is in Christ Jesus our Lord. (KJV)

Oh, how marvelous! Nothing can come between us, Father. I am so very grateful. Because of Your Love for me, no devil, no evil, no sin and not even death can stop You, my God, from loving me, Your Child. No situation, no circumstance, no time and no distance can keep You from loving me. You so loved me and the entire world, that You gave us a Savior. Your Desire is for no one to perish, but for all to come unto You. When they do, everlasting life is what they receive. This is such an Awesome Truth. Glory Hallelujah!

There is no power, principality or anything else that can keep You from loving me. Nothing can ever come between us, Almighty God.

Speaking God's Word

I am fully persuaded that as You love me today, Your Love for me will be the same tomorrow and forever. Hallelujah! There is no condemnation in me that comes from You. No matter what happens around me, no matter what I do, You will always love me. Thank You for Your Love that simply overwhelms me. There is no other like You, Father. You are Love!

Thank You, God for Your Unchanging Love. Thank You for not being double-minded. Thank You, God for loving me from the beginning to the end. I love You too! Because You are my Father and my Friend, I am more than a conqueror and I always win. I praise Your Name. You are God, You are Good, and You are always the same. Blessed be the Most High God – who is worthy to be praised. I bless Your Holy Name!

Love, Joy and Peace

Psalm 40:16

Let all those that seek thee rejoice and be glad in thee: let such as love thy salvation say continually, The LORD be magnified. (KJV)

But may the joy of the Lord be given to everyone who loves him and his salvation. May they constantly exclaim, "How great God is!" (TLB)

As I seek You, Lord, I find joy because of who You are and what You are to me. Where would I be without Your Salvation and Deliverance? Thank You for healing me too, Jehovah Rapha. Thank You for loving me and favoring me, unconditionally. Thank You for prospering me, Jehovah Jireh. You are a Great and Awesome God and I glorify Your name. You are my all in all. You are my everything. I rejoice continually because of Your Goodness and Mercy. You are my Savior. Hallelujah!

You are a Mighty Wonder and I will continually praise You. You are the Great and Magnificent El Shaddai and I exalt You. There is no other like You. You flood me with joy.

Speaking God's Word

I find absolute bliss in You always. I experience an overflow of laughter and delight from You. It cannot be explained. I fear not. I fret not. I just rejoice in You and remain full of praise. I announce to all I see, that You are the cause of my overwhelming glee!

You are a Great God. You have redeemed me from the curse of the law. Only You could love me enough to snatch me from the grips of the devil, to save me from the pit of hell. Only You could love me so much and make me so free. I just want to proclaim to the world, what a loving, mighty and good God You are to me. You are my Strength and my Shield. You are my Sustainer too. Lord Almighty, I just want to say thank You!

Love, Joy and Peace

John 14:27

Peace I leave with you, my peace I give unto you: not as the world giveth, give I unto you. Let not your heart be troubled, neither let it be afraid. (KJV)

Peace I leave with you; My [perfect] peace I give to you; not as the world gives do I give to you. Do not let your heart be troubled, nor let it be afraid. [Let My perfect peace calm you in every circumstance and give you courage and strength for every challenge.] (AMP)

Praise the Lord! I have peace that goes beyond anything I've ever known. Thank You, Father. When things don't seem to be going in the right direction, I do not fret. I do not fear. I will not be intimidated or unsettled. My heart is not troubled. I remain calm and courageous. You have given me peace that the world cannot and would not understand. I receive Your Strength for whatever challenge I may face. I am forever grateful, Father!

Glory be to God! When the world seems to be upside down and everything appears out of control, I have peace. Your Peace allows me to be fearless and know that all is well.

Speaking God's Word

Your Peace comforts me when it seems that all hell is breaking loose. Your Peace soothes my soul so that I smile and know that I am not alone. You are always with me, Jehovah Shammah. I am covered by the Blood of Jesus. I am at peace and nothing or no one can harm me.

Hallelujah! The world could never give me the peace that comes from You, Lord God. The temporary fix, the false solutions and the enticing activities of the world are not match for You. Your Peace allows me to walk boldly as a Child of God. Your Peace rests on me so that others want to know how could it be, that I am so happy and free. Thank You, Jesus, for Your Peace. You are the Prince of Peace!

Love, Joy and Peace

<u>Romans 15:13</u>

Now the God of hope fill you with all joy and peace in believing, that ye may abound in hope, through the power of the Holy Ghost. (KJV)

May the God of hope fill you with all joy and peace in believing [through the experience of your faith] that by the power of the Holy Spirit you will abound in hope and overflow with confidence in His promises. (AMP)

I am filled with joy and peace. Hallelujah! You are my God and You fill me with hope. My hope is in all that You have promised me. I believe Your Word. I believe Your Covenant. I believe in the Power of the Holy Spirit who dwells in me. I thank You, Father, for giving me peace. When trouble comes, You keep me at peace. There is nothing missing and all is well with me. Glory to You, Father!

I am filled with peace and unspeakable joy in the Holy Ghost. Because my hope is in You, I am not troubled by any circumstance or situation I may find myself in. Instead, I believe that my God, the God of Hope, will work it out.

Speaking God's Word

You always fill me with all the joy and all the peace I could ever require. You go beyond my expectations, Father. Every day I abound in hope and I overflow with confidence too. You have said yes and amen to all of Your Promises to me. Great joy is mine every day. Glory Hallelujah!

I am filled with the Holy Spirit and through His Power, I endure. I am confident in You and my expected end is assured. My hope is in You for every good thing. Your Kingdom in me is the source of my peace. Your Loving Kindness is the reason I am at peace. Your Faithfulness is what sustains my peace. Your Sovereignty keeps me at peace. Thank You, Your Majesty, for my soundness and health, my prosperity and wealth, and my joy and peace! You are more than enough for me!

Love, Joy and Peace

<u>Ephesians 5:1-2</u>

Therefore be imitators of God as dear children. And walk in love, as Christ also has loved us and given Himself for us, an offering and a sacrifice to God for a sweet-smelling aroma. (NKJV)

Follow God's example in everything you do just as a much loved child imitates his father. Be full of love for others, following the example of Christ who loved you and gave himself to God as a sacrifice to take away your sins. And God was pleased, for Christ's love for you was like sweet perfume to him. (TLB)

I choose this day to walk in love. As Your Child, I choose this day to imitate You, Father God. I choose this day to follow Your Example in everything I do. I desire to be just like You, Father. My goal is to copy Your Behavior as a Loving, Generous and Faithful Father. As Christ loved and gave Himself, I too am open and receptive for Your Purpose and Will to be done through me. Have Your Perfect Way with me, Father God.

I choose to honor You, Father, by loving everyone I meet. I will show empathy and compassion towards everyone.

Speaking God's Word

I will always be mindful of what is best for others. I will extend my love by praying for others. I am available to intercede for others. I shall always be willing to make up a hedge and stand in the gap for those whom You place on my heart. As You desire me to bring others to Your Throne of Grace and Mercy, I am willing, Father.

I choose to be Your Ambassador of Love and Peace in this earth. My intention is to do everything that would be pleasing to You, my Lord. My focus is to do unto others as I would have them do unto me. I am ever ready and prepared to offer comfort and consolation to anyone in need who crosses my path. I desire my love walk to be a sweet fragrance to You, my God.

Love, Joy and Peace

Psalm 4:8

I will both lie down in peace, and sleep; For You alone, O LORD, make me dwell in safety. (NKJV)

In peace I will lie down and sleep, for you alone, O LORD, will keep me safe. (NLT)

In peace [and with a tranquil heart] I will both lie down and sleep, For You alone, O LORD, make me dwell in safety and confident trust. (AMP)

I praise You, my Lord and thank You for peaceful sleep. How great You are to cover me with peace and safety, wherever I am. I lie down and sleep with a tranquil heart every night. Even in the midst of my enemies, I know that You are with me. I have no fear, no doubt, nor any anxiety about death, because You have promised me a long life. Thank You, Father. Hallelujah!

Only You, Lord, are able to secure me when I sleep. Only You, Lord, sustain and maintain me. Thank You for Your Awesome Promise to keep me safe, despite what may be going on around me. Sweet, peaceful sleep is what You give me.

Speaking God's Word

I thank You for being the Keeper of my Soul. I confidently trust You always. Thank You for never leaving me nor forsaking me. In You I live, move and have my being. For this, Father God, I am forever grateful!

You, Most High, are my dwelling place. I trust You, Almighty Father. Glory be to You, God. I am not afraid of any terror nor any darkness. I do not fear any kind of destruction nor disaster. I will never be devastated. Thank You, Lord God, for giving Your Angels charge over me. They keep me and my family in all our ways. You are a Great, Loving God. There is none above You. You are a Wonderful and Mighty God. You alone are able to guarantee my safety and my future. You reign! I praise Your Holy Name!

Love, Joy and Peace

NOTES & REFLECTIONS
COMMENTS & YOUR THOUGHTS
ON
LOVE, JOY AND PEACE

Speaking God's Word

_____

_____

_____

_____

_____

_____

_____

_____

_____

_____

_____

_____

_____

_____

_____

*W*isdom, *K*nowledge & *U*nderstanding

Wisdom, Knowledge & Understanding

<u>James 1:5</u>

If any of you lacks wisdom, let him ask of God, who gives to all liberally and without reproach, and it will be given to him. (NKJV)

If any of you lacks wisdom [to guide him through a decision or circumstance], he is to ask of [our benevolent] God, who gives to everyone generously and without rebuke or blame, and it will be given to him. (AMP)

How awesome You are, Father. You give me the wisdom I need – and all I have to do is ask. I thank You. When I am in a position of doubt or confusion, I turn to You and You flow through me with the wisdom that I require. You show me what to do and what not to do. You tell me how to do what is before me to accomplish. If I am in doubt, I do not look to others for answers. I ask of You, Father. You make things clear for me. You always give me an above only perspective of whatever circumstance or position I may be in. Thank You, God, for being such a Generous Father!

How awesome You are, Father. You do not judge or rebuke me when I need Your Help. You promised to withhold no good thing from me as I walk uprightly. I now know that this includes Your Wisdom. When I call unto You, You answer me and show me great and mighty things.

Hallelujah! You are the Omniscient God who knows everything there is to know. You are Omnipresent as well. You have all the wisdom and knowledge there is, and You are everywhere evenly present at the same time. This is simply wonderful. There is no information that You do not have because You are the Creator of the Universe. Thank You, Father!

Wisdom, Knowledge & Understanding

Proverbs 3:5-7

Trust in the Lord with all thine heart; and lean not unto thine own understanding. In all thy ways acknowledge Him, and He shall direct thy paths. Be not wise in thine own eyes: fear the Lord, and depart from evil. (KJV)

Lean on, trust in, and be confident in the Lord with all your heart and mind and do not rely on your own insight or understanding. In all your ways know, recognize, and acknowledge Him, and He will direct and make straight and plain your paths. Be not wise in your own eyes; reverently fear and worship the Lord and turn [entirely] away from evil. (AMPC)

I trust You, Lord, not only with my heart, but with everything. I submit to You in every way – what I should eat, what I should wear, where I should go, what I should do, to whom I should talk, and what I should say. I do not lean on my own, limited understanding. I acknowledge You always. When I arise in the morning, I seek You and Your Directions. Throughout the day I listen to hear Your Instructions. When I lie down to rest, I await Your Whispering to me any new thing that You desire me to know.

Speaking God's Word

I trust You, Lord. I do not rely on my own insight or understanding. I allow You to have Your Way. I do not yield to worldly knowledge or scientific facts. You are the All Powerful Omnipotent God and there is nothing or no one above You. Therefore, I simply trust You, Most High God, for I know that You always know what is best for me, Your Child.

I trust You, Lord. My confidence is in You and You alone. In everything that concerns me, I recognize You as the One who orders my steps. It is You who direct my path. It is You who straighten out the crooked places and smooth out all the rough edges in my life. I glorify You and I reverence You, Father God. I worship You. I exalt You and I praise Your Holy Name!

Wisdom, Knowledge & Understanding

John 16:13

However, when He, the Spirit of truth, has come, He will guide you into all truth; for He will not speak on His own authority, but whatever He hears He will speak; and He will tell you things to come. (NKJV)

When the Holy Spirit, who is truth, comes, he shall guide you into all truth, for he will not be presenting his own ideas, but will be passing on to you what he has heard. He will tell you about the future. (TLB)

Thank You, Holy Spirit, for living in me. I thank You for glorifying and magnifying Jesus Christ in me. I thank You for leading me, guiding me, and exalting the Word of God in me. What a blessing it is to have the Spirit of Truth teach and direct me. I can trust Him to give me the Truth and nothing but the Truth. I receive revelation of the Word because the Holy Spirit ministers to me. He unveils the Mysteries of the Kingdom of God to me. He counsels and corrects me too. Revelation knowledge comes to me as I listen and receive. Thank You for Your Awesome Presence. I honor You and I welcome You always!

Speaking God's Word

My future looks bright because the Holy Spirit gives me advance notice of things to come. He gives me fare warning of what to do and what not to do. I know where to go, and who and what to stay clear of because He tells me so. Father, You've seen my end from the beginning and guide me to my destiny.

How wonderful it is to know that everywhere I go, the Holy Spirit is already there. Everything that is before me to do, because of Him, I am fully prepared. I have been taught the Truth, I know what to expect, and I never despair. Hallelujah! There is nothing to compare. His guidance makes me happy and free. By Him I am grounded and directed, covered and protected. I do not need to confer with any outside forces. I have everything I need within me – the Whole Spirit of God. How Marvelous! Hallelujah! To God be all the Glory!

Wisdom, Knowledge & Understanding

Colossians 2:8

Beware lest any man spoil you through philosophy and vain deceit, after the tradition of men, after the rudiments of the world, and not after Christ. (KJV)

Don't let anyone capture you with empty philosophies and high-sounding nonsense that come from human thinking and from the spiritual powers of this world, rather than from Christ. (NLT)

I shall never again be caught up in the philosophies and intellectualism of other people. I shall not be deceived by any such nonsense or foolishness. I will not be lured into idle fancies or crude notions of what is the Truth. I have decided to follow Jesus. I will not allow anyone to beguile me with enticing words, other than Jesus Christ, Him crucified, and rose from the grave. I've decided to know the Truth and I have been set free indeed. I choose to follow the leadings of the Spirit of Truth and I can never go wrong. There is nothing to compare to the Word of God, which is the absolute, Highest Truth there is. Glory to God!

Speaking God's Word

I no longer put my trust in physical or material things. Rather, I trust in the invisible, spiritual and eternal, which is the highest reality. When I am faced with any decision, I do not confer with flesh and blood. I do not rely on scientific evidence from trial and error. I yield to the Holy Spirit and I never go wrong. I will not be tricked by Satan with any religious philosophies that suggest anything other than the Absolute Truth about who I am in Christ. No theological practice, human reasoning or any base, worldly teaching, can overrule, override or take the place of the Truth – that Jesus Christ is Lord. He is the Messiah! He is the King of Glory! Jesus Christ is the same yesterday, today and forever. Glory be to Jesus!

Wisdom, Knowledge & Understanding

Proverbs 2:6-7

For the LORD giveth wisdom: out of his mouth cometh knowledge and understanding. He layeth up sound wisdom for the righteous: he is a buckler to them that walk uprightly. (KJV)

For the Lord gives skillful and godly Wisdom; from His mouth come knowledge and understanding. He hides away sound and godly Wisdom and stores it for the righteous (those who are upright and in right standing with Him); He is a shield to those who walk uprightly and in integrity. (AMPC)

 For the Lord grants wisdom! His every word is a treasure of knowledge and understanding. He grants good sense to the godly—his saints. He is their shield, protecting them and guarding their pathway. (TLB)

Father, I eagerly accept the Wisdom You give me. I no longer think that I know it all. I seek Your Understanding for everything. When I find myself unsure of what to do, I call on You. Your Wisdom, Guidance and Instructions come through. When I am faced with a challenge, I know I can always trust that Your Knowledge will come forth through me. There is no mistake in Your Wisdom.

Speaking God's Word

Nothing is left out and there is no room for doubt. You are an expert in everything, Lord, and I am forever grateful.

I incline my ears to always listen. As I do, I follow Your Godly Wisdom. I always know what to do. I walk upright in a good and perfect relationship with You, and I maintain my integrity too. You are a shield to me. You are the Lord God Jehovah Tsidkenu. My righteousness comes from You.

Jehovah God, out of Your Mouth comes the only Wisdom and Knowledge I will ever require. I will forever treasure Your Word. I fully trust the sound, solid Wisdom that You have stored up for me since before the foundation of the world. I accept it, I believe it, I receive it. Your Wisdom, Your Knowledge and Your Understanding keep me safe, happy and free. Glory!

Wisdom, Knowledge & Understanding

1 Peter 4:11

If any man speak, let him speak as the oracles of God; if any man minister, let him do it as of the ability which God giveth: that God in all things may be glorified through Jesus Christ, to whom be praise and dominion for ever and ever. Amen. (KJV)

Whoever speaks, [let him do it as one who utters] oracles of God; whoever renders service, [let him do it] as with the strength which God furnishes abundantly, so that in all things God may be glorified through Jesus Christ (the Messiah). To Him be the glory and dominion forever and ever (through endless ages). Amen (so be it). (AMPC)

When I speak, I aim to speak as the Oracles of God. I shall speak as one who is well versed in the Word of God. I shall preach the gospel of the Kingdom of God. I shall teach those things which concern the Lord Jesus Christ with all confidence, and with no man forbidding me. My Words are precise, accurate and based on His Word. My speaking and teaching is to do one thing – to preach Christ. My speech and my preaching shall not be with enticing words from man's wisdom, but in demonstration of the Spirit and of Power. Thank You, Father. Glory be Jesus. Hallelujah!

Speaking God's Word

When I minister to others, I do so with the authority and the ability that God has given me. It is not of my own power that I give service to others, but from the strength that my God freely gives to me. My life of service is solely for the purpose of glorifying and magnifying El Elyon, the Most High God, through our Lord and Savior, Jesus Christ.

I thank You, Father God, for sending Jesus to fulfill Your Plan of Redemption. I am so thankful for Jesus that through His obedience, my relationship to You, God Almighty, has been restored. Heaven is real. The devil has been defeated. Jesus Christ is Lord. Our God is a good God, all the time. Amen!

Wisdom, Knowledge & Understanding

<u>Proverbs 3:13</u>

Happy is the man that findeth wisdom, and the man that getteth understanding. (KJV)

Joyful is the person who finds wisdom, the one who gains understanding. (NLT)

Happy (blessed, fortunate, enviable) is the man who finds skillful and godly Wisdom, and the man who gets understanding [drawing it forth from God's Word and life's experiences] (AMPC)

I am a happy child of God. I have good fortune in everything I do. Praise the Lord! I am never sad or discouraged. I find the wisdom I need in You, Father. I am happy indeed because when I seek Your Wisdom, it is not hidden from me. I no longer get upset or frustrated about anything. Any problem that arises in my life is easily solved because Your Understanding flows through me. I remain joyful and keep a smile on my face and in my heart. Hallelujah!

Thank You for giving me skillful and Godly wisdom. I get understanding every day for every situation – from You, Your Word and Your Instructions. Life is not hard for me.

Speaking God's Word

When I am in doubt – I turn within – You teach me and guide me and order my steps. Because I am connected to You, every obstacle before me is destroyed.

You know all there is to know, as the Omniscient God Almighty. You confound the wise ones of this world with foolish things. Yet I, as Your Child, am never confused. There is no mystery beyond my comprehension. You infuse me with wisdom and understanding whenever I need it. No task is too difficult for me and no solution ever evades me, because the Great Teacher, the Holy Spirit, indwells me. Glory be to God! I am therefore blessed, fortunate, enviable and so very happy and free. Selah!

Wisdom, Knowledge & Understanding

Ephesians 1:17-18

That the God of our Lord Jesus Christ, the Father of glory, may give unto you the spirit of wisdom and revelation in the knowledge of him: The eyes of your understanding being enlightened; that ye may know what is the hope of his calling, and what the riches of the glory of his inheritance in the saints. (KJV)

[For I always pray to] the God of our Lord Jesus Christ, the Father of glory, that He may grant you a spirit of wisdom and revelation [of insight into mysteries and secrets] in the [deep and intimate] knowledge of Him, By having the eyes of your heart flooded with light, so that you can know and understand the hope to which He has called you, and how rich is His glorious inheritance in the saints (His set-apart ones). (AMPC)

The God of my Lord Jesus Christ, the Father of Glory, has given me the spirit of wisdom and revelation in the knowledge of Him. My spiritual eyes – the eyes of my understanding – have been enlightened. Praise the Lord! I now know what is the hope of His calling for me. I understand what my glorious and rich inheritance is as a Child of God. I am one of His set apart ones. I have been sanctified and purified by the Blood of Jesus. My Lord! Glory Hallelujah!

Speaking God's Word

As a Spirit Filled Believer, I have the ability to speak in unknown tongues as the Holy Spirit gives utterance. When I do, I tap into the Mind of God and speak forth His Wisdom.

The Holy Spirit reveals all things to me. I have insight into the Mysteries and Secrets of the Kingdom of God. Solutions to problems are poured into my spirit. Questions are answered as revelation knowledge is released. What was hidden becomes unveiled for me. Glory to God! This is part of my inheritance that is available to me, and to all the Saints of God. Oh Praise His Name! Nothing is hidden, nothing is missing, nothing is lost and nothing is ever too complicated for me. Thank You, Father. Thank You, Jesus. Thank You, Holy Spirit. Thank You for insight and clarity!

Wisdom, Knowledge & Understanding
NOTES & REFLECTIONS
COMMENTS & YOUR THOUGHTS
ON
WISDOM, KNOWLEDGE AND
UNDERSTANDING

Speaking God's Word

*P*ower and *A*uthority

Power and Authority

<u>2 Samuel 22:33</u>

God is my strength and power: and he maketh my way perfect. (KJV)

God is my strong Fortress; He guides the blameless in His way and sets him free. (AMPC)

My Lord! You, Father God, are my Strength, my Power, and my Strong Tower. You have given me the ability to go forward. When I feel like stopping and saying "no more" You urge me to keep going. You assure me that I am not alone and to continue on. You encourage me to proceed with confidence because You've already made my way perfect. You've already gone ahead of me to clear the path for me to follow. How marvelous You are to me!

My Lord! You have not only provided a place of protection for me, but You are indeed my Fortress. You are my help in times of trouble. You make me safe and fortify me with all I require. I am a conqueror because You are my God.

Speaking God's Word

Nothing or no one can stand in my way or stop me because of who You are. You are a Supernatural God with Supernatural Power and Abilities. You strengthen me and set me free. Hallelujah, victory belongs to me. Thank You, Jehovah Nissi!

My Lord! You have perfected everything concerning me. How can I thank You for being so good to me? As You guide and direct my path, I know that I am always safe, because You make no mistakes. I relax in You, Father. You are my God and my Protector. You are my Shield and my Refuge. I trust You, Lord. Through Your Power and Your Strength, You always keep me covered and protected, and out of harm's way. You reign forever. You alone are God!

Power and Authority

Luke 10:19

Behold, I give unto you power to tread on serpents and scorpions, and over all the power of the enemy: and nothing shall by any means hurt you. (KJV)

Behold! I have given you authority and power to trample upon serpents and scorpions, and [physical and mental strength and ability] over all the power that the enemy [possesses]; and nothing shall in any way harm you. (AMPC)

Look out devil. In the Name of Jesus, I have not only been given authority, but I have been given all power over you, and all of your evil agents. You have no more authority over me. You no longer have permission to operate in my life. At every turn, I rebuke your destructive forces and do not give in to your temptations, lies and suggestions. I have the Blood of Jesus flowing through my veins. Over you I rule and reign!

This day I take authority over the spirit of infirmity and refuse its operation in my mind and body as pain, sickness, disease or depression. This day I exercise my power over you, Satan, and cancel every one of your attacks, plots and schemes.

Speaking God's Word

Today is the day that I rise up and take my position – above you always. I resist your interference, your diabolical plans, your evil intentions, and your harassment against me and my life, forever!

Heavenly Father, Your Expectation is for me to totally trample on and annihilate all of Satan's influence and opposition. The power and ability to subdue his forces, to thwart his assignments, and to destroy his activities against me are mine – through Jesus Christ! Thank You, God. I use this power and ability to defeat the devil in whatever form he shows up. I walk in my authority and dominion. The devil is defeated and I am victorious. I take full control over Satan now, in the Name of Jesus Christ of Nazareth. Amen!

Power and Authority

<u>Deuteronomy 8:18</u>

But thou shalt remember the LORD thy God: for it is he that giveth thee power to get wealth, that he may establish his covenant which he sware unto thy fathers, as it is this day. (KJV)

Remember the LORD your God. He is the one who gives you power to be successful, in order to fulfill the covenant he confirmed to your ancestors with an oath. (NLT)

I will keep thanksgiving and praise on my lips, and gratitude in my heart. I will always remember and acknowledge You, Lord God, as the source of my wealth and success. Thank You for being such a Gracious Father. The power and ability to be all that You have created me to be comes from You. It is through You that I make progress in all areas of my life. It is through You that I am able to persevere and accomplish my goals. With You I shall reach my destiny.

Lord God, thank You for giving me the power and privilege to acquire wealth, for Your Purpose and Your Plan. Acquiring Covenant Wealth to establish Your Kingdom here on the earth is therefore my purpose and plan as well.

Speaking God's Word

You always teach me to profit and bless the works of my hands. Therefore, everything that I touch is destined to increase. All that is before me to do shall be successful, because of Your Power working in and through me.

Father God, all respect and honor belong to You for giving me the power to get wealth. You gave it so that You may confirm Your Covenant, which You have sworn and promised. It is with great joy and happiness that I live my life for You. My sole purpose is to do everything that I have been created to do, and to participate and flow in Covenant Agreement with You. I shall live my days in obedience and eat the good of the land. You are a Covenant Keeper. You are a Great God. You are a Mighty God. You are my God. Hallelujah!

Power and Authority

<u>Acts 1:8</u>

But you shall receive power when the Holy Spirit has come upon you; and you shall be witnesses to Me in Jerusalem, and in all Judea and Samaria, and to the end of the earth. (NKJV)

But you will receive power and ability when the Holy Spirit comes upon you; and you will be My witnesses [to tell people about Me] both in Jerusalem and in all Judea, and Samaria, and even to the ends of the earth. (AMP)

Thank You, Jesus. As one of Your disciples and joint heirs too, I receive the Power and Ability of the Holy Spirit. I am a witness for You. I shall indeed spread the Glorious Gospel of Jesus Christ. Thank You for the extraordinarily Awesome Gift of the Holy Spirit. It is my pleasure to teach and preach the Good News, Jesus. Although You were crucified and buried, on that third day You rose again. Hallelujah! Death could not hold You down. You are alive today, living in the hearts of all those who believe in You. All shall know about You, Jesus. Thank You for Power and Authority. Thank You for defeating Satan at Calvary and giving me the victory!

Speaking God's Word

Thank You, Jesus, for being my Advocate with the Father and my High Priest too. Glory to You, Jesus, my Savior and Deliverer. You are the only Mediator between the Father and me. You are the Bread of Life, and my Best Friend. You are the First and the Last, the Beginning and the End. You are the Good Shepherd and the Rock of my life. Thank You, Jesus for not only being the Messiah, but the Way, the Truth and the Life. You are the Risen King and You Reign Supreme. You are the Holy Lord of All. Hallelujah, You picked us up from the Fall. As the Holy Spirit empowers me, I will let the whole world know, that You are the Lamb of God and so much more. Glory to You, Jesus!

Power and Authority

Revelation 12:10-11

And I heard a loud voice saying in heaven, Now is come salvation, and strength, and the kingdom of our God, and the power of his Christ: for the accuser of our brethren is cast down, which accused them before our God day and night. And they overcame him by the blood of the Lamb, and by the word of their testimony; and they loved not their lives unto the death. (KJV)

I overcome Satan by the Blood of the Lamb and by the word of my testimony. As a Born Again Believer, I have been given the power and authority to overcome any and everything that Satan brings against me. Thank You, Father. The victory has already been given to me. Jesus died on the cross, defeated the devil and took back everything for me. Therefore, when the accuser of the brethren spews out lies and condemnation toward me, I overcome him by the word of my testimony, that Jesus Christ is Lord!

I let the devil know that by His Stripes I am healed. I inform him that through the Blood of Jesus, I have been saved, delivered and set free, with full authority.

Speaking God's Word

I testify that I belong to Christ and have been reconciled with Almighty God. I say to him that salvation, strength and power have been given to me through Jesus Christ. I testify to the Truth that Christ became poor on the cross so that I might be made rich. Hallelujah, the devil is a liar and Jesus is the Messiah!

I testify that I have been made in the image and likeness of the Most High God, and given dominion on this earth. I proclaim to that foul mouth fool that none of the weapons he tries to use against me will succeed. I am the Righteousness of God which is my heritage. Hallelujah! I further inform him that I have been empowered with the Indwelling Presence of the Holy Ghost. That same life giving, death defeating Spirit that raised Christ from the dead, now lives in me. Selah!

Power and Authority

Luke 17:6

And the Lord said, If ye had faith as a grain of mustard seed, ye might say unto this sycamine tree, Be thou plucked up by the root, and be thou planted in the sea; and it should obey you. (KJV)

If your faith were only the size of a mustard seed," Jesus answered, "it would be large enough to uproot that mulberry tree over there and send it hurtling into the sea! Your command would bring immediate results! (TLB)

I do indeed have faith the size of a mustard seed, so when I speak to things, they obey. Thank You, Lord. I have been given a measure of faith by God, my Father. Therefore, I speak to every circumstance and every condition that appears in my life that I do not desire – and they obey me. They obey my voice of authority. I thank You for this empowerment, Lord. I am a Child of the Most High. Hallelujah! Glory be to God!

Thank You, Father, for giving me the authority to speak to things. I have a voice of power and authority to speak to any problem. When I speak to storms, they must obey me.

Speaking God's Word

When I speak to pain and sickness, they too must bow to my command. When I speak to my body, it yields to my words. When I speak to my finances they obey – and do what I say. I just thank You, Father. Hallelujah! Glory be to God!

Thank You, Father, for putting death and life in the power of my tongue. I speak life and declare that I shall live and not die. You have given me the authority and ability to speak blessings or curses. I choose blessings, Father. I therefore speak a blessing to everyone I meet. Thank You, Father, for such a powerful ability that You have given to me. Praise the Lord! As I speak with the authority given me, it (whatever it may be) obeys me. Thank You, Father. Hallelujah! Glory be to God!

Power and Authority

<u>Mark 16:17-18</u>

And these signs shall follow them that believe; In my name shall they cast out devils; they shall speak with new tongues; They shall take up serpents; and if they drink any deadly thing, it shall not hurt them; they shall lay hands on the sick, and they shall recover. (KJV)

These signs will accompany those who have believed: in My name they will cast out demons, they will speak in new tongues; they will pick up serpents, and if they drink anything deadly, it will not hurt them; they will lay hands on the sick, and they will get well. (AMP)

Praise the Lord! I am a Believer. I therefore have signs following me. I have the ability to cast out demons, in the Name of Jesus. What a powerful mandate You have given, Lord. There is no fear because nothing or no one can hurt me. Thank You, Jesus, for Your Healing Presence which continues through me, as a Believer. Glory to God. I praise Your Holy Name, Jesus!

Hallelujah, Lord! I believe Your Word, Jesus. I boldly speak in new tongues. I have been made for signs and wonders.

Speaking God's Word

There are no impossibilities with You. Just as You healed them all then, You are still healing all today. Therefore, there are no incurable diseases because You are Jesus Christ, The Healer. You are the same yesterday, today and forever. You are Lord!

I proceed and follow Your Commandments, Jesus. I lay hands on the sick and expect them to recover. I speak to demons, and command that they leave those who are being tormented. When I do, they obey me and come out – because I have no doubt. Thank You, Jesus, for making all those things that seem impossible possible. Thank You, Father God, for desiring all to be in good health and have strong minds. Glory Hallelujah! You are Awesome!

Power and Authority

Where the word of a king is, there is power: and who may say unto him, What doest thou? (KJV)

For the word of a king is authoritative and powerful, And who will say to him, "What are you doing?" (AMP)

The king's command is backed by great power, and no one can withstand it or question it. (TLB)

As a Citizen of the Kingdom of God, my words are authoritative and powerful. Through the Grace of God and His Gift of Righteousness, I am in right standing with God, my Father. I have been given the right and ability to reign in life through Jesus Christ. He is the King of Kings and Lord of Lords. How Wonderful! I am one of those kings and a lord too. Glory Hallelujah!

As one with Royal standing, I have the awesome and powerful ability to make decrees. When my words are released, they shall not return to me void. I have the right to decree a thing and, according to the Promise of God, my decrees shall be established for me.

Speaking God's Word

Not only that, the Light of God's Favor shines upon me in all my ways. My commands are backed by great power – the Power of God Almighty. Praise the Lord!

Glory Hallelujah! I am a Child of God and an heir of salvation. Therefore, the authority of my word shall not be questioned. When I speak, angels assigned to minister to me are listening for my words – to carry out my commands for me. I am surely Royalty. Thank You, Father, for creating Your Children to rule and reign on this earth. You are an Awesome God! Thank You for creating us to have total dominion, in Jesus's Name, Amen!

Power and Authority

Matthew 16:19

And I will give you the keys of the Kingdom of Heaven. Whatever you forbid on earth will be forbidden in heaven, and whatever you permit on earth will be permitted in heaven. (NLT)

I will give you the keys (authority) of the kingdom of heaven; and whatever you bind [forbid, declare to be improper and unlawful] on earth will have [already] been bound in heaven, and whatever you loose [permit, declare lawful] on earth will have [already] been loosed in heaven. (AMP)

Glory to God! I have been given the Keys of the Kingdom of Heaven. I have the authority to bind what I do not want and loose what I want to have instead. Thank You, Jesus. What an awesome power! As a Born Again Believer, whatever I bind or forbid here on earth will be bound and forbidden in heaven, and whatever I loose or permit on earth will be permitted in heaven. This is absolutely wonderful. I can declare as improper and unlawful anything the devil would try to bring against me, and into my life. When I do, it will indeed be bound and forbidden. Likewise, I have the power to loose or allow all of heaven's best to be released in my life. Hallelujah!

Speaking God's Word

Glory to God! Satan, in the Name of Jesus, I rebuke you, all of your demonic forces and every one of your evil works. I bind every diabolical attack on my mind, body and affairs. I forbid from coming to pass any act of witchcraft or sorcery against me. I cancel all satanic assignments with my name on them. Devil, I do not permit any of your traps, schemes or plots to manifest in any area my life.

The Yoke Breaking, Burden Removing Anointing of Jesus Christ operates in and through me. I declare that by His Stripes I am healed. I have been saved, delivered and set free. I am covered by His Blood. I loose the Power and Protection of Almighty God to surround me like a shield. I permit the Grace, Favor and Mercy of God to operate in my life. I accept and expect the Blessing of the Lord to be upon me always, in everything I do and everywhere I go. It is so, in the Name of Jesus. Amen and Amen!

Power and Authority

_____

_____

_____

_____

_____

_____

_____

_____

_____

_____

_____

_____

_____

Speaking God's Word

*F*aith and *F*aithfulness

Faith and Faithfulness

<u>Romans 12:3</u>

For I say, through the grace given to me, to everyone who is among you, not to think of himself more highly than he ought to think, but to think soberly, as God has dealt to each one a measure of faith. (NKJV)

For by the grace [of God] given to me I say to everyone of you not to think more highly of himself [and of his importance and ability] than he ought to think; but to think so as to have sound judgment, as God has apportioned to each a degree of faith [and a purpose designed for service]. (AMP)

Thank You for Your Grace, Father. Thank You for the Faith You have given me. I realize that of my own self, I can do nothing. I remain steadfast and sober in You, Father God, and do not place myself higher than I should. I realize that I live, move and have my being in You. I am Your Offspring, made in Your Image and Your Likeness. It is through Your Faith in me that I can call things that be not as though they were. By Your Grace, I am above only and never beneath. I am the head always and never the tail. I am of Your Royal Priesthood. I am a winner. I always succeed!

Speaking God's Word

You have given me a measure of Your Faith. Praise the Lord! I have the Faith of God operating in and through me. Therefore, all things are possible for me. Through the Faith of God, I can do all things!

Thank You for endowing me with Your Mountain Moving Faith. Continue to lead and direct my life and impart Your Plans and Directions to me, Father. As You do, I will follow. I shall serve others and remain focused on the purpose You have created me for. Thank You for empowering me with the faith to do all things that are before me to do. Glory to You, Father. You are an Amazing God!

Faith and Faithfulness

2 Corinthians 5:7

For we walk by faith, not by sight. (KJV)

For we live by believing and not by seeing. (NLT)

For we walk by faith [we regulate our lives and conduct ourselves by our conviction or belief respecting man's relationship to God and divine things, with trust and holy fervor; thus we walk] not by sight or appearance. (AMPC)

I follow Your Command, Father – to walk by faith and not by appearances. No longer will I just settle for what I can see. Because I walk by faith and not by sight, I am living the way You would have me to live – by faith. I have faith in You. I believe that You are my God and I am Your Child. My life is regulated by faith. I now realize that what I cannot see with my natural eyes is more real than what is appearing before me now. Never again will I be limited by what I see. Thank You, Father!

Every day I am determined to rise to a higher level and move toward what has been promised me. I have faith in our Covenant, Father. I've made a decision to use my faith to bring about changes in my life.

Speaking God's Word

I stand in faith and pursue what I believe is mine. I shall have what belongs to me. I will not quit. My faith in the divine spiritual realm propels me forward and I shall reach my destiny. When I'm unsure of which way to go, my faith acts as a force, that opens up the door. Thank You, Father!

I am determined not to focus on appearances. I have faith in what is not seen. I conduct my daily affairs accordingly. My faith – the substance of what I hope for – becomes the evidence of what I am expecting. Whatever it is, it shows up all the time, because I walk by faith and not by sight. My life is a life of faith. I accept it. I believe and I receive. Thank You, Father!

Faith and Faithfulness

1 Thessalonians 5:24

Faithful is he that calleth you, who also will do it. (KJV)

God will make this happen, for he who calls you is faithful. (NLT)

Faithful is He Who is calling you [to Himself] and utterly trustworthy, and He will also do it [fulfill His call by hallowing and keeping you]. (AMPC)

Thank You, Father God, for always seeing me through. You hold me together when I want to give up. You comfort me and tell me to hold on, it won't be long. When I'm about to fall, You keep me upright, so that I see the light. When I think it's over, You tell me to get up, to go further. You assure me not to give in. I trust You and You always cause me to win. If You, Father God, are for me, then nothing or no one can stand against me. Thank You for Your Faithfulness!

Thank You for keeping me out of harm's way, my Lord. I am so grateful that You did not give up on me. You have not changed Your Mind about me.

97

Speaking God's Word

Thank You for calling me for Your Plan and Purpose for my life. I praise You, Father, for being forever faithful to me. I could not have made it this far without You. I will never ever try to do anything without Your Help, Your Guidance and Your Support. I've come this far by my faith in You. Thank You, Lord! I call You Faithful because You are Faithful indeed!

Thank You for calling me to be Yours. You are my Refuge and my Portion, Oh Faithful God. When the going gets tough, I trust You to pick me up. You are always there and carry me through. I will always depend on You. I press toward the mark for the prize of the high calling. Christ in me is my hope of glory. I move toward my destiny. I triumph and have the victory. As You keep me, cover me and hold my hand, I shall indeed reach my promised land. Thank You, my Faithful Father!

Faith and Faithfulness

<u>Hebrews 11:6</u>

But without faith it is impossible to please Him: for he that cometh to God must believe that he is, and that he is a rewarder of them that diligently seek him. (KJV)

But without faith it is impossible to [walk with God and] please Him, for whoever comes [near] to God must [necessarily] believe that God exists and that He rewards those who [earnestly and diligently] seek Him. (AMP)

My desire is to please You, Father. I believe with all my heart that You are God Almighty, Creator of Heaven and Earth. You are my Father and I am Your Child. I know without a doubt that You supply all of my need according to Your Glorious Riches. I have faith in You, God. I have faith in Your Word. I have faith in our Covenant. You are not a man that You should lie. I come before You, Father, with complete confidence that You always hear me, and always answer my requests. I diligently seek You, Father, for everything. I wish to please You and You alone. I seek my reward from You and You give to me freely and abundantly. You alone are El Shaddai!

Speaking God's Word

My desire is to delight You, Father. I am sold out for You. I believe that You are the Alpha and the Omega. You are my God, my Lord and my Provider. You are my everything. I trust You to be the Source of all that I wish. You in turn honor me with the desires of my heart. You reward me with Your Faithfulness. You bless me with Your Presence. You have given me Your Free Gift of Grace, which is my sufficiency. You have infused me with Your Power and Authority. You love me because You are Love. You have given me the right and privilege to walk and talk with You. You are truly a Faithful Father. I worship and adore You. You are my Reward. A Great and Awesome and Mighty God You are!

Faith and Faithfulness

Romans 4:19-20

And being not weak in faith, he considered not his own body now dead, when he was about an hundred years old, neither yet the deadness of Sarah's womb: He staggered not at the promise of God through unbelief; but was strong in faith, giving glory to God; (KJV)

And Abraham's faith did not weaken, even though, at about 100 years of age, he figured his body was as good as dead—and so was Sarah's womb. Abraham never wavered in believing God's promise. In fact, his faith grew stronger, and in this he brought glory to God. (NLT)

I too am growing stronger and stronger in faith. I have made a decision to stand and believe. No matter what the facts are in the natural, I will not waiver. I believe in the Promises of God. As I grow in faith, I am empowered and strengthened. I receive Your Promise to me, Abba Father. Although it may seem impossible, I know that nothing is impossible for me, because there are no impossibilities with You. You are the Supernatural God of the Miraculous and I am Your Child!

Speaking God's Word

I've made a decision to remain firm in my faith, and I will not go back. I shall not change my mind. I no longer allow unbelief in my heart. I am finished being double minded. I call things into being because I believe the Word of God. I remain fixed in my faith in You. I trust You and I trust our Covenant. You are the Infallible, Faithful God. You said it, I believe it, and I receive it. Glory be to God!

As a Seed of Abraham through Christ Jesus, I aspire and strive to have no unbelief about the Promises of God. I will not doubt or question You and Your Word, God. NO unbelief! I am encouraged and excited. I will not try to figure out how it will happen. I will watch and see how You manifest Your Promises to and through me. As I grow stronger in my faith, I want to bring Glory to You, Father God, because all Glory and Honor belong to You and You only!

Faith and Faithfulness

Mark 11:22-24

So Jesus answered and said to them, "Have faith in God. For assuredly, I say to you, whoever says to this mountain, 'Be removed and be cast into the sea,' and does not doubt in his heart, but believes that those things he says will be done, he will have whatever he says. Therefore I say to you, whatever things you ask when you pray, believe that you receive them, and you will have them. (NKJV)

I am whoever. Thank You, God for showing no partiality or favoritism among Your Children. My faith is in what my God is able to do. I have faith in You and faith in Your Word. I follow Your Directions and I say what it is that I want. When I do, I am exercising my faith. I speak what I desire to have, and what I desire to change. At the time that I pray is when I believe I receive. I believe that I have what I have prayed for. What an awesome promise and ability You have given me. Glory Hallelujah!

I am whoever and I do not doubt in my heart – in my spirit. I diligently push any thoughts of doubt out. I replace all doubt and unbelief with faith – faith in God and faith in what I speak.

Speaking God's Word

I have faith and I believe. Whatever I have spoken and decreed – everything that I have released with my mouth – will come to pass – without a doubt. It will happen. I have faith that I have whatever I say. I believe Your Word because I have faith in You. You are God who cannot lie. Hallelujah!

I am whoever and I can have whatever I say. If I speak it, it will come to pass. It will manifest. I have faith in Your Immeasurable Power, Father. I have faith and assurance that as You have spoken it, it shall happen for me. According to my faith it is done unto me. How awesome. How wonderful. What a great God You are. Glory Hallelujah!

Faith and Faithfulness

<u>Hebrews 10:23</u>

Let us hold fast the profession of our faith without wavering; (for he is faithful that promised;) (KJV)

Let us seize and hold tightly the confession of our hope without wavering, for He who promised is reliable and trustworthy and faithful [to His word]; (AMP)

I will not let go of my profession of faith. I will not waiver or give in. I will say what You have said in Your Word, Father. I will proclaim with my mouth what thus sayeth the Lord. With my mouth I will openly announce and admit the Truth about my situation, as written in the Scriptures. I declare in faith that Jesus is Lord. I profess that I am a Child of El Shaddai, the Almighty, Self-Sufficient God. I acknowledge that I and my Father are one – there is no separation. I confess that the Presence of God is with me always. Hallelujah!

I will not let go of my confession of faith. I will follow and obey what You have said for me to do. I give evidence of my faith by the words that I speak.

Speaking God's Word

I will keep the Word of God in my mouth at all times. As I do, I will make my way prosperous and I will have continuous success. Glory Hallelujah! Thank You for these simple instructions. I will make known Your Word – and tell others how good You are. You are Reliable, Trustworthy and Faithful – all the time. What a Mighty God!

I will hold fast to my faith, and my declaration of it at all times. You are the One, Father, who backs up Your Word. You are the One who hastens to perform Your Word. Your Word will not return to You void. Likewise, Your Word will not return to me void either. Your Word accomplishes what It is sent to do, and succeeds in doing what It is intended to do. Yes and Amen, Father!

Faith and Faithfulness

<u>Romans 10:17</u>

So then faith comes by hearing, and hearing by the word of God. (NKJV)

So faith comes from hearing, that is, hearing the Good News about Christ. (NLT)

Hallelujah! My faith comes by hearing Your Word, Father. Hearing the unadulterated Word of God is what I seek. I accept nothing less than the Word of God to operate in my life. The Word of God causes me to have faith. Hearing what You have said about who and what I am in You causes my faith to increase. I am not only a hearer of Your Word, Father, but I am a doer of Your Word. I do what You tell me to do. I tithe and I thrive. I give and I receive. I love and I am loved. I forgive and I am forgiven.

Father God, I plant Your Word as seed into my heart. As a result, the Truth of who I am in You grows and develops in me. I am indeed a new creation. Hearing the Word that Jesus Christ, Him crucified, has changed my life. Praise the Lord!

Speaking God's Word

He did it all for me. I have a new destiny. My sins have been forgiven and I have been redeemed from the curse. Hearing Your Promises for me and my life causes me to see things differently. I no longer depend on the distorted world view to dictate my way of living. My expectation for everything is in You and You alone.

I allow the Word of God to mold and shape my life. I look to You, Father God, as my Source and my Provider. You are my Creator and my Sustainer. You are my Protector and my Deliverer. You have a Covenant with me to bless me and make my name great. You are my Father and I am Your Child. Heaven and Earth will pass away but Your Word will never fail. For this I give You alone all the glory, all the praise and all the honor, forever. Amen!

Faith and Faithfulness

Then touched he their eyes, saying, According to your faith be it unto you. (KJV)

Then he touched their eyes and said, "Because of your faith, it will happen." (NLT)

According to my faith be it unto me. I have confidence that what I hope for will happen. I have assurance about the things I cannot see. I have no doubt, running about. You have given me this ability. Thank You, Father. According to my faith I will succeed in the things that I have been assigned to do. I won't confer with flesh and blood. Rather, I will just follow the directions and leadings of the Holy Spirit and believe that those things will come to pass.

Because of my faith, I receive healing in my body. Because of my faith, when I pray for others, Jesus Christ heals them too. Hallelujah! My faith in You encourages me to obey Your Voice, Father God.

Speaking God's Word

When I receive Your Instructions, I simply follow them. I trust You, Almighty Father. I am so pleased that You always know better than I, because You have declared the end from the beginning. I therefore place my faith in You – to see me through. Thank You, Father, because You always do. My God! You are Forever Faithful!

According to my faith I accept all of Your Promises, Father God. You have already said yes and amen. It is up to me to believe and receive. I tap into the realm of unlimited possibilities with my faith. I will not give up and I will not give in. I will receive my inheritance and reach my promised land. My mind is made up and I am going on in. My faith will take me there to fulfill Gods' Plan. According to my faith I shall reach my destiny – and collect all of the things that belong to me!

Faith and Faithfulness

NOTES & REFLECTIONS
COMMENTS & YOUR THOUGHTS
ON
FAITH AND FAITHFULNESS

Speaking God's Word

Thoughts and Thinking

Thoughts and Thinking

Proverbs 23:7

For as he thinks in his heart, so is he. 'Eat and drink!' he says to you, but his heart is not with you. (NKJV)

Glory to God! I am what I think. What I think becomes what I believe, and what I believe manifests in my life. Therefore, my life experience is what I make it. I choose to think about who I am in Christ. In Him I am complete, happy and free. I am what I think about all day long. I am always victorious. I am a winner. Nothing is ever impossible for me. I have great expectations, Father God. My expectations are from You. In You there are no shortages or limitations, and there is no lack of any kind. In You all things are possible. Hallelujah!

I refuse to allow evil thoughts to proceed out of my heart. I will not be defiled by foul thinking. I manage my thought life because I know that the issues of life flow out of me. I focus on the Word of God. I refuse to think that God's way of doing things is too hard for me. I keep my mind stayed on the Truth of who I am. I am a wealthy, healthy, ageless, Born

Speaking God's Word

Again Believer. I am the head and not the tail, always on top and never beneath. I am always successful!

I keep my soul intact. I do not allow my thoughts to run rampant. I maintain control of my mind, my will, my imagination, as well as my emotions. I am not moved by oppressive thoughts from the evil one. My thoughts exude my true identity. I am favored of the Lord. I am all that. I am a Kingdom Citizen. I am a champion. I am a divine spiritual being. I am living a life of grace. I choose to always think highly of myself because I belong to Highest One!

Thoughts and Thinking

Philippians 4:8

Finally, brethren, whatsoever things are true, whatsoever things are honest, whatsoever things are just, whatsoever things are pure, whatsoever things are lovely, whatsoever things are of good report; if there be any virtue, and if there be any praise, think on these things. (KJV)

Thank You, Father, for these instructions. I will focus on Your Goodness all the time. I will not allow my thoughts to wander aimlessly. I will think and meditate on what is true, which is Your Word and Your Word only. Lord, if it goes against Your Word, I will not dwell on it. I keep my mind under control. I quench every fiery dart and take authority over every demonic thought the devil sends my way. I bring them all under captivity to the obedience of Christ.

Satan and his twisted system are full of lies and trickery. But, I, as a Believer, recognize his deception. I now know who I am. My true identity is in Christ. I have a far above mind-set. I will only accept the Truth and not dwell on any falsehoods from this moment on.

Speaking God's Word

I focus on what You've already done for me. I rest in Your Finished Work, Father God. You have already delivered me, healed me and saved me from the pit of hell. I've been set free to walk triumphantly. There is no going back. My future is set. I concentrate on these things. Praise the Lord! Hallelujah!

I keep my mind out of the gutter and refuse to allow garbage in. I do not allow ungodly strongholds to taint my thinking. I keep my standards high and maintain my integrity. I focus on what is pure, honest and good. I strive for excellence in everything that I do. I radiate only the highest and the best, and I therefore attract only the highest and the best to me. I seek out what is admirable in others and only expect and accept a good report. Thank You for these instructions, Father. They are not too hard for me. I shall indeed follow them always. Amen!

Thoughts and Thinking

<u>James 1:8</u>

A double minded man is unstable in all his ways. (KJV)

[For being as he is] a man of two minds (hesitating, dubious, irresolute), [he is] unstable and unreliable and uncertain about everything [he things, feels, decides]. (AMPC)

Their loyalty is divided between God and the world, and they are unstable in everything they do. (NLT)

I will not waiver. I will not be double minded. I remain stable and sound in all my ways. I choose to follow what You say, Lord. My communication is clear. When I say yes, I mean yes. When I say no, that's exactly what I mean. I make a decision and I stick with it. I imitate You, Father God. When You say yes, You mean yes. You do not go back on Your Word and neither do I.

I commit my ways unto You, Heavenly Father. My activities and affairs are unto You. I am mindful of You and Your Heart. What matters to You is what is important to me. I'm about Your Business – to expand the Kingdom of God right here on the earth.

Speaking God's Word

I no longer entertain worldly thought patterns. I trust You to establish my thoughts so that I will never look back. I will not go back and forth. I will not hesitate. I will remain reliable and stable. My loyalty is with You always, my God.

I will not be double minded. My days of being wishy-washy are over. My soul is fixed on You. It is settled. I've made my decision. There will be no low plan for my life. Everything is alright for me. I choose to forget the past. That old person that I was no longer exists. Hallelujah! I keep my mind stayed on You and my future looks bright. I move forward towards Your High Calling. Jesus is King! Jesus is Lord! Period.

Thoughts and Thinking

Proverbs 30:32

If thou hast done foolishly in lifting up thyself, or if thou hast thought evil, lay thine hand upon thy mouth. (KJV)

If evil and foolish thoughts cross my mind, I cover my mouth and do not allow them to come out. I control my tongue and shut my mouth. I manage my mind and I guard my thoughts. I realize that my thoughts turn into my beliefs, and whatever it is that I believe, will be my experience – it will show up in my life. Therefore, if boastful or arrogant thoughts try to overtake me, I remember that it is You and You alone, Father God, who is worthy to be praised. All Glory belongs to You!

Thank You God for how You have created me. I understand that I cannot separate my thoughts from how I am living. My inner thoughts overflow and establish my outer life. I keep watch over my mouth and do not let any wrong thoughts come out. Out of my mouth comes blessings or curses. I choose blessings. From this day forward, I am diligent about what I say. I will only allow what is pure and honest to come forth out of this mouth.

Speaking God's Word

I desire to love life and see good days. Therefore, I will not sin with my tongue. I will bridle my tongue at all times. I refrain from releasing evil words. I will not allow any haughty or proud talk to be used as a weapon against me. I will not invite accidents and tragedies, or sickness and disease to come upon me – by agreeing with the enemy. Instead, I will choose words to keep me safe. I will speak with Godly wisdom so that my speech is respected by others. I choose to speak life to every situation, so that my words are always pleasing to You, Abba Father.

Thoughts and Thinking

Romans 12:2

And be not conformed to this world: but be ye transformed by the renewing of your mind, that ye may prove what is that good, and acceptable, and perfect, will of God. (KJV)

Don't copy the behavior and customs of this world, but let God transform you into a new person by changing the way you think. Then you will learn to know God's will for you, which is good and pleasing and perfect. (NLT)

I will not be conformed to this world. I am being transformed day by day to Your Will and Your Way of doing things, Father. As a Saved Child of the Holy Lord God, my instructions are to have my mind renewed to what Your Word says. I no longer have the right to think or act any kind of way, or to copy the behavior and customs of Satan's corrupt world system. I am under orders to renew my mind and I obey!

As a new creature in Christ Jesus, I allow my inner man to be renewed day by day. I choose to believe the Word of God and what It says about me.

Speaking God's Word

Father, I believe that Your Will for me is good and very good, all the time. I accept that Your Plan for my life is perfect. Hallelujah! I don't have to look to the world to know how to live each day. I do not act like the world. I do not do what the world's system says I should do. I follow the guidance of the Holy Spirit, who is my Best Teacher. Praise the Lord!

As a renewed spiritual being, I do not depend on anything that the world would offer me. I already know my status, my worth and my identity. I am no longer impressed by media influence. I do not care to follow the lives of the rich and famous who are not living a saved and sanctified life, no matter who they are. I trust You, Lord Jesus, to change me into the person who I was created to be. I am being transformed by the Word of God and I am very happy about the new me. Hallelujah!

Thoughts and Thinking

Philippians 2:5

Let this mind be in you, which was also in Christ Jesus. (KJV)

Let this same attitude and purpose and [humble] mind be in you which was in Christ Jesus: [Let Him be your example in humility:]. (AMPC)

Let the Mind of Christ be in me. Glory be to God. I have the Mind of Christ. I choose to have His same attitude and purpose. Let the same spirit of humility be in me as well. He is the living God dwelling in me. I can now rise up above natural thoughts. When I was born again into the Kingdom of God, I received the Creative Mind of Christ. I have the ability to transcend human thoughts and limitations. I therefore refuse to allow myself to wallow in the natural because I know that there is so much more. How awesome!

I have been reborn into the Supernatural Kingdom of the Most High God. I therefore make it my business to be guided and instructed by His Thoughts and Purposes. I harness my thoughts and keep them steady and stable. I refuse to be scattered in my mind.

Speaking God's Word

I will keep focused on the Mission and Plan of God for my life. I will not be stiff-necked, but I will yield to the Word of God and His Instructions. I keep my mind stayed on Jesus.

I am made in the image and likeness of God Himself. Therefore, I am a limitless creation with total dominion and authority here on the earth. I have the ability to create. I can call things that be not as though they were, and expect that they show up, and they do. Praise God, I am created this way, just like my Father. I am an extraordinary, one of a kind being, who can do all things through Christ Jesus who lives in me!

Thoughts and Thinking

Proverbs 12:5

The thoughts of the righteous are right: but the counsels of the wicked are deceit. (KJV)

A good man's mind is filled with honest thoughts; an evil man's mind is crammed with lies. (TLB)

The thoughts and purposes of the [consistently] righteous are just (honest, reliable), But the counsels and schemes of the wicked are deceitful. (AMP)

As one who has been made the Righteous of God through Jesus Christ, I keep my thoughts right and honest. I do not allow Satan to pervade my mind with evil thoughts of any kind. I govern my thoughts and keep them centered on what is good, just and reliable. I think about the Truth that there is one God and one Father who is above all, and one Lord Jesus Christ. I am mindful of the Covenant between me and God Almighty. He is my Father and I am His Child. He loads me daily with benefits and is the Restorer of my soul. Glory Hallelujah!

Speaking God's Word

Expand my ability to comprehend what You have already done for me, Father God. I commit my works unto You always, so that my thoughts are established by You. I do not bow to deceitful counsels and wicked schemes of the devil. No longer will I be desensitized to the Truth by the deceptions and lies from Satan. Glory to God, I will never again be tricked by him. I clear the atmosphere of any negativity with my thoughts, and resist any attempt to be influenced otherwise. I keep my mind focused on the Truth that nothing is impossible with God so nothing is impossible for me. My thoughts are centered on who my God is to me – good, faithful, trustworthy, reliable, dependable and loving. Thank You, Father. I love You. I bless You. I appreciate You. You are Wonderful. You are Marvelous. You are Awesome!

Thoughts and Thinking

Jeremiah 29:11

For I know the. thoughts that I think toward you, saith the LORD, thoughts of peace, and not of evil, to give you an expected end. (KJV)

For I know the plans and thoughts that I have for you, says the LORD, plans for peace and well-being and not for disaster to give you a future and a hope. (AMP)

My God! I receive Your Thoughts and Plans for me. You are an Awesome God. Thank You for loving me. Thank You for creating me and keeping me on Your Mind. You have had plans for my life since before the foundation of the world. How marvelous You are. Your Warm and Kind Thoughts and Plans for my peace and well-being are so soothing to me. In You I have hope and a future because no disaster shall come upon me. What an Extraordinarily Great God You are. Hallelujah!

My God! You formed me and knew me while I was yet in my mother's womb. How precious are Your Thoughts to me, Lord. Your Thoughts are so high and lofty toward me and my life. Wow!

Speaking God's Word

I just thank You. Your Desire is not to bring any harm to me, but for me to have an expected end that is good and very good. Hallelujah! I thank You and I praise Your Name!

My God! My future looks bright. My hope and trust is in You and You alone. Thank You for providing everything that I will ever need or require in my life. It is already prearranged, prepared, and set for me – as I move toward my destiny. It is so pleasing that You take care of me in Your very own special way, Father. You have me in Your Hands. The Thoughts of Your Heart are for me and for all generations. You are such a Great Provider. You are the Almighty God. I worship and exalt You. I praise You and I bless Your Holy Name forever! Selah!

Thoughts and Thinking

NOTES & REFLECTIONS
COMMENTS & YOUR THOUGHTS
ON
THOUGHTS AND THINKING

Speaking God's Word

Sonship

Sonship

<u>Galatians 3:26-29</u>

For ye are all the children of God by faith in Christ Jesus. For as many of you as have been baptized unto Christ have put on Christ. There is neither Jew nor Greek, there is neither bond nor free, there is neither male nor female: for ye are all one in Christ Jesus. And if ye be Christ's, then are ye Abraham's seed, and heirs according to the promise. (KJV)

I am a Child of God. I have been reborn from above. Praise the Lord, I have been spiritually transformed. I have been sanctified and set apart for God's Purpose. Through my faith in Jesus Christ, I have been renewed and restored. I have been baptized in Christ. I am clothed in Christ and He now lives in me. Hallelujah to the Lamb of God. I belong to Jesus Christ, the King of Majesty. What an honor!

I am a seed of Abraham. The God of Abraham is my God too. I am blessed with faithful Abraham, wherever I am. As Abraham believed, so do I. What You did for Abraham, Father, You have done for me as well. Thank You.

Speaking God's Word

I am a Friend of God. Hallelujah! I am in Covenant with You, too. No limit, no exception, no shortage and no restriction. You are a Rich God to all who call upon You. Thank You for being such a Glorious and Great God!

I am an heir of God and a joint heir with Christ Jesus. Hallelujah! Whatever belongs to Jesus belongs to me. The earth is the Lord's and the fullness thereof, so I have inherited the whole earth too. How awesome You are to me, Father. What a Mighty God You are. In every area of my life, I have success because You have given me the victory. You have said yes, yes, yes. Every one of Your Promises belong to me! I bless Your Holy Name! Hallelujah!

Sonship

John 1:12

But as many as received him, to them gave he power to become the sons of God, even to them that believe on his name. (KJV)

But to as many as did receive and welcome Him, He gave the right [the authority, the privilege] to become children of God, that is, to those who believe in (adhere to, trust in, and rely on) His name. (AMP)

Jesus Christ is the Way, the Truth and the Life. Hallelujah! I have received You in my life, Jesus. I open my mouth and say – to all who have ears to hear – that Jesus is my Lord! I thank You for giving me the right, the authority and the power to become a Child of God. What a privilege. I believe in Your Name. Thank You, Jesus. Salvation comes only through Your Name and Your Name alone. It the Sweetest Name I know. There is none other. Thank You, Jesus!

Jesus Christ is the firstborn of God. I am one of the children too. I receive Jesus into my life totally. Glory be to God. Thank You for choosing me. I am a Believer. I believe what the Word of God says.

Speaking God's Word

I adhere to, I trust and I rely on the Name of Jesus. Yours is the Name above all names. It is something about the Name of Jesus. Hallelujah! There is power in the Name of Jesus. Jesus! Jesus! Jesus!

Jesus Christ is the King of Kings, the Lord of Lords. Every knee must bow and every tongue shall confess that Jesus Christ is Lord. There is none other. I thank You, Jesus, for the privilege of knowing You. Thank You, Jesus for being joined together with me. I am blessed to be called a son of God. I have been regenerated and restored to my position of royalty. I walk in my divinity. I am grateful that You chose me. Praise the Lord! I am a Child of the Most High God, and I am extremely proud to be Yours! Glory, Glory, Glory!

Sonship

Philippians 2:14-15

Do all things without murmurings and disputings: That ye may be blameless and harmless, the sons of God, without rebuke, in the midst of a crooked and perverse nation, among whom ye shine as lights in the world; (KJV)

Do everything without complaining and arguing, so that no one can criticize you. Live clean, innocent lives as children of God, shining like bright lights in a world full of crooked and perverse people. (NLT)

What a privilege it is to be a Child of God. I honor You, Father, by being obedient to Your Call. I honor You, Father God, by eagerly doing what is before me to do, without murmuring or complaining. I keep my tongue under control. As Your Representative here on the earth, I desire to shine as one of Your Lights – a Child of God. Hallelujah! You are the Magnificent One!

What an honor it is to have the opportunity to call You my Father. I therefore do everything for Your Approval. From important assignments to the most menial tasks, I do all to the Glory of God.

Speaking God's Word

I choose to live a life to make You proud of me. I guard my eyes from filth. I do not allow profane or corrupt words to come into my ears or proceed out of my mouth. I strive to stand out in this perverse and sinful world, to Your Delight!

What a responsibility You have given me. Thank You for trusting me to be a light in this world. I live my life for You and for You alone. Since I belong to You, I am respectful to everyone I meet. I keep strife out of my relationships. I avoid bickering, arguing and nit-picking. I stay clear of situations and activities that give the appearance of anything less than what You expect of me – the highest and the best. My hope is that my behavior, the words of my mouth, and the meditation of my heart are acceptable to You, my God!

Sonship

Ephesians 2:10

For we are his workmanship, created in Christ Jesus unto good works, which God hath before ordained that we should walk in them. (KJV)

For we are His workmanship [His own master work, a work of art], created in Christ Jesus [reborn from above— spiritually transformed, renewed, ready to be used] for good works, which God prepared [for us] beforehand [taking paths which He set], so that we would walk in them [living the good life which He prearranged and made ready for us]. (AMP)

I have been born again from above. I am a spirit being, created for the supernatural. Thank You, Father God, for creating me for good works. I walk in Your Prophetic Plan and Purpose. Thank You for ordering my steps so that when I veer off the path, You gently push me back into the way You would have me to go. I thank You, Father, because Your Way is always good and very good. I thank You because Your Way is not hard. I thank You for prearranging everything for me. My Goodness! My God!

141

Speaking God's Word

Father, I choose to live the life of promise – the good life. I choose to live the life that Jesus made available for me – a life of abundance. You have created me to prosper and to be in health. You said that I am the Apple of Your Eye. Not only that, You have raised me up to sit with You in Heavenly Places. You shower me with Your Grace and Favor, Your Love and Kindness, Your Splendor and Your Exceeding Riches through Christ Jesus. Hallelujah! What a God!

As Your Child, I thank You for knowing everything about me. I am delighted that You will never turn Your Back on me. I am grateful to You for always making a way out of nowhere for me, and for keeping me on track. I accept the call to be used by You and to represent You as Your Workmanship. It's all for Your Glory, Father!

Sonship

1 John 3:1

Behold, what manner of love the Father hath bestowed upon us, that we should be called the sons of God: therefore the world knoweth us not, because it knew him not. (KJV)

See what [an incredible] quality of love the Father has given (shown, bestowed on) us, that we should [be permitted to] be named and called and counted the children of God! And so we are! The reason that the world does not know (recognize, acknowledge) us is that it does not know (recognize, acknowledge) Him. (AMPC)

For Your Love, I honor and adore You, Father. For making me Yours, I just magnify and glorify Your Name. You are the Great I Am. Hallelujah! How awesome it is that You would allow me to be called and counted as one of Your Children. I am no longer ignorant to my identity. I believe it and I receive it. I know it and I show it. Thank You for Your Goodness, Most Awesome God!

As Your Favorite Child, I decide to fully accept and act like who I am. I no longer pretend to be anything else other than the splitting image of You, my Father.

Speaking God's Word

I am a spiritual being who has a supernatural Father. I'm a Citizen of the Kingdom of God. I am in this world but not of this world. I have been transformed by the Word of God and I'm extremely grateful and glad about it. When they see me, Father, they see You! Glory Hallelujah!

As You love me, Father, I simply cherish You. You are an Amazing Father. You are Jehovah Rapha, my Healer and Jehovah Jireh, my Provider. You are El Shaddai, the Almighty God and Jehovah M'Kaddesh, my Sanctifier. You are El Olam, the Everlasting God and Jehovah Saboath, the Lord of Hosts. You are Alpha and Omega, the Beginning and the End. Adonai, my Lord, You are all that and so much more. You are the One whom I worship and adore. Hallelujah! I magnify You and praise Your Holy Name!

Sonship

Romans 8:17

And if we are [His] children, then we are [His] heirs also: heirs of God and fellow heirs with Christ [sharing His inheritance with Him]; only we must share His suffering if we are to share His glory. (AMPC)

I am an heir of God. My inheritance in Christ is therefore massive. My inheritance is immeasurable. My inheritance is limitless. Hallelujah! The earth is the Lord's. Therefore, this earth belongs to me too. Since I am a Child of God and joint-heir with Jesus, everything that He has is mine as well. I am an heir to prosperity. Healing is my birthright. I am an heir to peace. I have inherited protection. I am covered under the Blood of Jesus. I am no longer available to the devil for I am free indeed. Glory to God!

I am an heir of God. Everything that Jesus has belongs to me too! Hallelujah! I share in the divinity of God. What a grand plan and what a great God. Everything that I could ever need, want or desire was provided for me before the foundation of the world.

Speaking God's Word

You are the Omnipresent, Supernatural God, and I am Your Child. You are the Beginning and the End. You knew me before I was even born. You set in place all things for life and godliness for me. You have made me Your Very Own and endowed me with all things I could ever require in this life here, on the earth. Thank You, Father God!

I am an heir of God. I am a co-heir with Christ Jesus. I am a member of God's Royal Family. You are worthy to be praised, Jesus. Thank You for securing my inheritance for me. I now have the power, riches, wisdom, strength, honor, glory and blessing that was stolen from me by the devil. You took it all back. Hallelujah! I take ownership now. Thank You for restoring me to my rightful position of Sonship. Thank You, Jesus! Glory be to God!

Sonship

<u>2 Peter 1:3-4</u>

According as his divine power hath given unto us all things that pertain unto life and godliness, through the knowledge of him that hath called us to glory and virtue: Whereby are given unto us exceeding great and precious promises: that by these ye might be partakers of the divine nature, having escaped the corruption that is in the world through lust. (KJV)

According to Your Divine Power, Father, You have provided me with all things that I could ever need, want, or desire for this life. Thank You, Lord. I am blessed to know You. I am even more blessed that You have called me to partake in Your Marvelous Glory, Your Virtue, and Your Excellence. I accept Your Unlimited Good in every area of my life. There are no limits to what I can have, what I can do, and what I can be. Hallelujah! I fully participate. Thank You, Father!

You've created me with the privilege of having Your Divine Nature. I must be in the God Class. I am Royalty! You're an Awesome God to make me in Your Image and Likeness. Thank You for giving me access to the Holy Spirit, Your Power here on the earth.

Speaking God's Word

As an heir of salvation, You have assigned angels to work for me as ministering spirits. Overwhelming excitement and honor is what I feel when I think about Your Goodness and Your Splendor!

Yes, Father! I partake of Your Divine Nature and accept all of Your Precious Promises. Yes, Father! I believe Your Word. I receive in my spirit that You have already given me everything required for life and godliness. I have them now. I call them forth now. You have already said yes and amen. I shall partake in all that belongs to me. I shall have my share of wealth and health. I shall walk in grace and favor, and experience uncommon joy and peace. Your Everlasting Love and Divine Protection belong to me. You are Amazing. I magnify You. I adore You. I praise You. I exalt You. I thank You, Lord!

Sonship

1 John 4:4

Ye are of God, little children, and have overcome them: because greater is he that is in you, than he that is in the world. (KJV)

Little children, you are of God [you belong to Him] and have [already] defeated and overcome them [the agents of the antichrist], because He Who lives in you is greater (mightier) than he who is in the world. (AMPC)

I belong to El Elyon, the Most High God. Hallelujah! My body is the Temple of the Holy Spirit. I have the Power of Jesus Christ in me. The Kingdom of God is within me. The One who has defeated Satan – the same One who was raised from the dead – is right here with me. Thank You, Lord God, for such an awesome plan. The One whom I seek and the One whom I worship lives on the inside of me. Father God, You are all I will ever need, and I will forever glorify and magnify You!

I belong to the High and Lofty God. Hallelujah! The devil is eternally defeated, along with all of his lying, evil agents.

Speaking God's Word

Therefore, when he raises his ugly head and comes against me, I do not fear. I have the Greater One on my side. I am not afraid of any terror by day nor by night. I do not have any dread of disease or disaster. I thank You, God. If You be for me, who can be against me? You reign! Thank You, Your Excellency. You are God Almighty!

I am of God. I am always victorious. I am of God. I walk in boldness. Nothing or no one can hurt me or bring me to destruction. I am equipped with the Holy Spirit of God living on the inside of me. From this day forward, I remain courageous and operate in my authority – as a Child of God and a Kingdom Citizen. I know who I am and whose I am. No devil in hell shall trespass or prevail against me ever again – in Jesus's Name!

Sonship

Psalm 82:6

I have said, Ye are gods; and all of you are children of the Most High. (KJV)

I have called you all "gods" and "sons of the Most High." (TLB)

Glory be to God! I am a Child of the Most High – a god, just like my Father. I have been created to operate just like Him, because I am His offspring. That is who I am. That is my identity – a Child of God. What a privilege. What an honor. What a birthright. There is no more doubt running about. Those of us who have been born again into the Family of God have been made to rule and reign here on the earth. We have been given dominion over everything on the earth – for the purpose of being on top and successful – as His Royal Children. We have been made just like Him – the Most High God, Creator of Heaven and Earth. Thank You, Your Majesty! Glory Hallelujah!

Glory be to God! I do not take my true birthright and worth lightly. As Your Child, Father, I have a big responsibility. I help those in need. I represent You in every way. I keep the enemy at bay. I will not die as a mere man, for I belong to the Royal King. I am in the God Class. Hallelujah! Glory be to God! I shall live the life You have prepared for me – a glorious, abundant and fruitful life – for all to see. I exude health, wealth and prosperity. I will not walk in darkness anymore. Instead, I will allow Your Light to shine through me. I am indeed one of Your Own – a god-like offspring with full authority. Hallelujah!

Glory be to God! I've been created as an invincible, unstoppable and uncommon being. I am a champion too. I am indeed limitless, happy and free, like You created me to be. Father, all I really want is You. You are my Reward. I keep my focus on Your Throne. I bow down, worship and honor You. I simply adore and appreciate You. You are more than enough for me. You are God Almighty. Glory Hallelujah!

Sonship

153

Speaking God's Word

Conclusion

I hope that you have enjoyed this book. As you speak and confess the scriptures, you will be planting the Word of God into your spirit. God, in turn, can perform His Word in your life. Remember, God says in <u>Jeremiah 1:12</u> *"for I will hasten my word to perform it."* Just as He was then, He is still listening for His Word to come out of our mouths, so that He can perform what we say. I urge you to have total trust and confidence that He is listening, waiting and ready to manifest Himself in a mighty way in your life.

I pray that an overflowing of God's Promises manifest in your life speedily, in Jesus's Name, Amen. God bless you!

ADDITIONAL NOTES, COMMENTS, THOUGHTS & RELATED SCRIPTURES

*S*alvation *P*rayer

If you are reading this book and have not accepted Jesus as your Lord and Savior, or you do not have a personal relationship with Him, or if you are unsure as to your status should you die today, then I encourage you to pray this prayer today:

"Heavenly Father, I come to You in the Name of Your Son, Jesus Christ. You said in Your Word that whosoever shall call upon the Name of the Lord shall be saved. I am calling on Jesus right now. I believe He died on the cross for my sins and that He was raised from the grave on the third day and is alive right now.

Lord Jesus, I am asking You to come into my heart now. I repent of my sins and surrender myself completely to You. I am asking You to live Your life in and through me.

Heavenly Father, I now confess Jesus as my new Lord and Savior from this day forward and I dedicate my life to serving Him."

Welcome to the Family of God!

157

About the Author

Gloria Moody, along with her husband, Ezell, founded Confessing God's Word Ministries in 2008. During that time, Gloria also released her first book *Speaking God's Word: A Book of Lessons and Confessions, Volume I.* It has been highly acclaimed and used as a biblical reference and study guide for several prayer and study groups.

Gloria walks in the Office of Pastor and Teacher in the Fivefold Ministry Gifts. The "Confessing God's Word Radio Broadcast" was launched in Chicago in 2009 and aired as a weekly teaching, and continued in the Pensacola, FL area through 2015. The program presented Word-based lesson sermons & teachings. Since 2010, the Ministry has also offered bible classes, prayer clinics, and prayer groups. Confessing God's Word Ministries held regular services from 2011-2015. Minister Moody also teaches & ministers at workshops, retreats, conferences, and other events.

Minister Moody is a graduate of Living Word Christian Center School of Ministry. Confessing God's Word Ministries is a member of the Faith Ministries Alliance, a spiritual covering under the leadership of Dr. Bill Winston and Living Word Christian Center in Forest Park, IL, where she was Ordained as a Minister of the Gospel in 2013.

Additionally, Gloria holds a Master's Degree in Multi-Categorical Special Education from Saint Xavier University in Chicago, IL; a Bachelor's Degree in Human Development-Behavioral Studies from Governors State University in University Park, IL.

Like us on our Facebook Page

"Speaking God's Word: A Book of Lessons and Confessions"

FOR FURTHER INFORMATION, VISIT US AT

www.speakinggodsword.org
or
www.confessinggodsword.org